SAMSON GICHUKI

Victorious Living

A 90-Day Devotional For Spiritual Growth

First published by GREAT Books 2020

Copyright © 2020 by Samson Gichuki

All rights reserved. No part of this publication may be reproduced, stored or transmitted in any form or by any means, electronic, mechanical, photocopying, recording, scanning, or otherwise without written permission from the publisher. It is illegal to copy this book, post it to a website, or distribute it by any other means without permission.

Samson Gichuki asserts the moral right to be identified as the author of this work.

Scripture taken from the New King James Version®. Copyright © 1982 by Thomas Nelson. Used by permission. All rights reserved.

First edition

This book was professionally typeset on Reedsy. Find out more at reedsy.com

To my Pastor Rev. Lucy Ware, my best friend and mentor, Mr. Waiyaki, and my entire JCA church family, you all have helped me grow spiritually and develop as a person.

To my friend Roy Kamau, were it not for your encouragement and support as I write, I wouldn't have completed this book.

To Jesus Christ, through your death on the cross, though many years ago, you saved me and delivered my soul from the darkness of sin and conveyed me into the light of your kingdom. Your love is real in my life.

Contents

Introduction		vi
A Prayer For You		vii

I God's Love

1	Infinite Love of God	3
2	Universal and Personal Love	5
3	Marked by God's Love	7
4	Embraced by God's Love	9
5	God's Love: A Marvelous Exchange	11
6	A Love That Brings True Freedom	13
7	You Got To Love	15

II God's Grace

8	Grace: The Backbone of Christianity	19
9	Grace: The Great Door-Opener	21
10	Grace: God In Action	23
11	Grace: Speaks Of Our Worth	25
12	Grace Shaped Identity	27
13	Limitations Removed By Grace	29
14	Sufficient Grace	31
15	Grace In A Real World	33

III God's Peace

16	Source Of Peace	37
17	Nature Of Peace	39
18	Governed By Peace	41
19	Guarded By Peace	43
20	Purse Peace	45
21	Guided By Peace	47
22	Peace Produced By The Spirit	49
23	Fruits Of Peace	51

IV Confidence in God

24	Because Of The Love Of God	55
25	Christ Centered Confidence	57
26	Source Of Strength	59
27	God's Opinion	61
28	Confidence In God	63
29	Confidence Through Jesus' Provision	65
30	Encouraged Through Faith And Love	67
31	Hiding Places	69
32	Worry Doesn't Work	71

V Walks Of Victory

33	The Ways Of God	75
34	A Worthy Walk	77
35	Your Attitude And Your Walk	79
36	Your Hearing And Your Walk	81
37	Depth And Impact	83
38	God Positioning System	85
39	Your Walk. Your Success	87
40	Don't Be Distracted	89
41	Memorial Stones	91
42	Testimony Triggers	93

VI Growth In God

43	Spiritual Priming	97
44	Protect The Foundation	99
45	Indicators For Growth	101
46	True Measure Of Faith	103
47	Guaranteed Growth	105
48	Breakthroughs	107
49	Growth Through Unity	109
50	Completeness	111

VII God's Promises

51	Assured Promises	115
52	The Best Promise	117
53	I Will Answer You	119
54	I Will Be Your Strength	121
55	I Will Be Your Provider	123
56	I Will Be With You	125

VIII   Identity In God

57	Brand R.G. – Righteousness of God	129
58	Your Identity And Calling	131
59	Your Identity: Your Conduct	133
60	Identity: Targeted	135
61	Renewed Identity. Renewed Thinking	137
62	Designed Unique	139
63	Created For God's Work	141

IX   Stewardship, Relationship, & Serving

64	Stewardship	145
65	Serving And Stewardship	147
66	Succeeding God's Way	149
67	Serving And Succeeding	151
68	Apostle's Paul Thoughts On Serving	153
69	Your Love, Treasures, And Heart	155
70	Sacrifice, Commitment, And Value	157

X	Victorious Warfare	
71	Understanding Warfare	161
72	Underlying Principles	163
73	Apply First-principles Strategy	165
74	God's Strategy	167
75	The Word of God	169
76	Godly Counsel	171
77	A Name With Authority	173
78	God's Presence Your Fortress	175
79	Safety In The Secret Place	177
80	Danger To Your Calling	179
81	Vision, Patience And Trust	181

XI	Satisfying and Fulfilling Life	
82	Reflecting On God's Goodness	185
83	No Wasted Experiences	187
84	Gratitude: An Attitude Changer	189
85	Humility: Promote Unity And Blessings	191
86	Seeing Value in Others	193
87	God Dependency - Trust	195
88	Your Fellowship. Your Fulfilment	197
89	Your Productivity, Your Fulfilment	199
90	Source Of Permanent Satisfaction	201
91	Equipped And Loaded For Victory (Bonus)	203

Introduction

Often, as children of a Mighty God, we lead a life far beneath what God intended for us to live. We fall victim to the deception of Satan, whose main agenda is to make sure we do not realize the power we have in Jesus Christ. Satan wants you to forget that it is in Christ you live and move and have your being.

When God looks at us, His beloved children, He sees us, men and women; young and old; educated and uneducated, living beneath our potential; He sees us not taking full advantage of who we are in Him; and also He sees that our unbelief is preventing us from fully exercising our full mandate here on earth.

When God created us, He wanted us to be victorious and live our best lives. He wanted us to have fellowship with Him and have access to His power. God did not call us into existence like He did the trees, or the animals but rather He looked into Himself as a prototype. He wanted us to be in His image and likeness so that we would have authority and dominion over everything on earth. In addition to our special creation, God blessed us with the ability to produce and increase.

The goal for this 90-day devotional is to help you see the love, blessings, and grace God has over your life; so that you grow and learn to develop others through serving; It is to guide you into living the life God had in mind for you - a victorious life.

A Prayer For You

According to Paul's prayer in Colossians 1:9-14, I pray that God will fill you with the knowledge of His will through all the wisdom and understanding that the Spirit gives. So that you may live a life worthy of the Lord and please Him in every way: bearing fruit in every good work, growing in the knowledge of God. That you be strengthened with all power according to His glorious might so that you may have great endurance and patience, giving joyful thanks to the Father, who has qualified you to share in the inheritance of His holy people in the kingdom of light. For He has rescued us from the dominion of darkness and brought us into the kingdom of the Son He loves, in whom we have redemption, the forgiveness of sins. Because of God, a victorious life awaits you.

    Amen.

I

God's Love

"In this, the love of God was manifested toward us, that God has sent His only begotten Son into the world, that we might live through Him. In this is love, not that we loved God, but that He loved us and sent His Son to be the propitiation for our sins. Beloved, if God so loved us, we also ought to love one another."
1 John 4:9-11

1

Infinite Love of God

The human mind can only understand what has a beginning and an end. In mathematics, we use the symbol of infinity to denote the point beyond our counting ability. The sky is the furthest our naked eyes can see. Our human nature can only deal with the finite matters of our universe, which gets in the way when we want to understand God, using our natural-self, especially understanding God's love.

While sin is the furthest 'distance' we can go from God, it has an end to it. God's love is more profound and broader than our understanding. Apostle Paul's prayer for the church of Ephesians was that they might be able to comprehend with all the saints what *is* the width and length and depth and height of the Love of God; to know the love of Christ which passes knowledge; that they may be filled with all the fullness of God (Ephesians 3:18-19). This prayer reveals that we can only grasp the vastness, richness, and depth of God's love through God's help. Paul says it's beyond knowledge. It explains why it doesn't make sense when you try to reason how God can forgive you your sins (small and big in our eyes). God's love replaces justice for mercy and condemnation for grace. Paul, who was the church's chief persecutor, was transformed to be the chief Apostle to the Gentiles. God loved us before we knew Him. Scripture says, "God demonstrates His own love toward us, in that while we were still sinners, Christ died for us" Romans 5:8.

The fact is, there is nothing you can do for God to stop loving you. Therefore, never allow the lies of the enemy to tell you that God's love is limited for you.

Reflection

- What is it in your life, you have done, that you think God's love can't cover?
- *Before you did what you did, God Loved you according to John 3:16.*
- Can you trust God and lean on His unfailing Love?
- What is stopping you from embracing God's Love?
- *Pray about it. Prayer shuts down all the lies of the devil that prevents people from embracing God's Love*

2

Universal and Personal Love

"For God so loved the world that He gave His only begotten Son, that whoever believes in Him should not perish but have everlasting life"
John 3:16.

The most joyous revelation is understanding how personal God's love is. When God is seated on His throne, He thinks about you and me; He desires to be in fellowship with us. His outpouring of love is so mighty that it changed our destiny forever when it came down on earth. The penalty of sin was the condemnation of man and the universe. Thereby to reverse this course, God's love had to be universal and personal.

The grandest gesture of love was when God chose His own Son to lay down His life to redeem you and me. I am convinced that when Jesus was hanging on the cross, He was thinking of us. The omniscient nature of God means that He was thinking about you when His only begotten Son was carrying the weight of the world and paying for all our sins through His precious blood.

While God poured His love and made it available for the whole world, we are to make a personal decision to believe in Jesus to personalize God's love and what it offers: everlasting life. When we choose Jesus, God's love becomes real to us; you experience it in a way that gives you a testimony that is unique as your life.

How do you choose Jesus? Revelation 3:20 holds the answer; it says, *"Behold, I stand at the door and knock. If anyone hears My voice and opens the door, I will come into him and dine with him, and he with me."* When you open your heart to Jesus, it shows your acceptance of His outstretched love through His Son. By this, the love that changed the world begins to work in you.

Reflection

- Have you accepted Jesus as the only Son of God?
- *When you accept Jesus into your life, you learn how to fully take advantage of God's love.*
- Why does Jesus want your heart?
- *Read Proverbs 4:23; Jeremiah 17:9.*

3

Marked by God's Love

In marketing, the labeling of commodities is a critical manufacturing step. Consumers often judge the quality of a product by its label. A poorly designed label will translate to low sales. While labeling is only on the surface, it creates a unique appearance of the products and sets an expectation of quality. The effect of labeling is enormous. It influences the choices of consumers.

In the spiritual world, labeling carries even greater weight. As children of God, that is, His offspring, we are branded to stand out. The scripture in 1 John 4:7 indicates that the one way to know that we are of God, born of God, or God's product is by love. A love-filled heart is the mark of a child of God. As God's kingdom envoys on earth, we are to radiate God's love; our actions, our speech, and our movements are supposed to be seasoned with love.

As a commodity that is a best seller or one that everyone wants to own or use, when we are marked with God's love, we become attractive to others. Apostle Paul referred to love as the bond of perfection. It's only by love that you can deliver what your Christian label states: tender mercies, kindness, humility, meekness, longsuffering; bearing with one another, and forgiving one another (Colossians 3:12-14).

So, as a believer, you will have the greatest impact here on earth if you're labeled and marked by God's love. Love is a powerful magnet that pulls the world to God, and we are privileged to be the point of contact for God's love through Christ to the world.

Reflection

- The only way to give something is if you have something. To give love, you must have received love. What are some things in your life that remind you of God's love?
- *When you are constantly sensitive to God's Love by remembering what He has done to you and for you, you will also continuously reflect that love.*

4

Embraced by God's Love

If you are a parent or have a younger sibling or have ever been in a position of taking care of people, you might have noticed one thing: the more you embrace them, the better they become. This is more evident in children. If you embrace them with your love, they can do unthinkable things; their courage increases, and their fear diminishes; they try things they would otherwise be shy to do. These propensities of embrace serve as a clue to what God's embrace does to His children (you and me).

The devil's resume contains three job titles: a robber, a killer, and a destroyer. The first goal of the enemy is to steal you from God's embrace. But he CANNOT do it by himself (without your help). So, he tricks you into thinking that God's embrace isn't enough. While the truth is that there is no embrace stronger than God's embrace for His Children; it is unbreakable. He hugs us so tightly that nothing can come between Him and us, not unless we walk away. Prophet Jeremiah proclaimed that God loves with an everlasting love (Jer 31:3), David sang and said, *"the Lord is merciful and gracious, slow to anger and abounding in steadfast love"* Psalm 103:8, and Apostle Paul asked, *"Who shall separate us from the love of Christ?...nothing shall separate us from the love of God in Christ Jesus our Lord"* Rom 8:35-39.

Therefore, the moment the enemy tries to make you feel not loved either because of something you did or how things are going, remind yourself that God's everlasting love is surrounding you.

Reflection

- In 1 Peter 5:8, we are warned to be sober since the devil is walking like a lion looking for someone to devour. Are there things, such as alcohol or busyness of life, that are making you unsober, failing to see the tricks of the devil that try to pull you out of God's embrace?
- What systems do you have in place such as prayer, reading of the Word, or fellowship with other believers, that will help you remain grounded in God's embrace?

5

God's Love: A Marvelous Exchange

Now cornered, with heavy, cold, and rusty chains on his ankles, he is sitting on a dusty floor in almost total darkness at the farthest corner of a windowless room. With little light coming through cracks in the door, he stares at the inscriptions on the walls from prisoners who came before him. Knowing his fate was going to be the most painful and humiliating death possible, he waits hopelessly. But his attention is drawn to the footsteps approaching. The door opens, and another man is thrown into the room while he is called out. To his greatest surprise, his chains are removed and he is set free because the other man is going to take his position on the execution line.

Barabbas was notorious; he had done heinous crimes and was set to be crucified. But his life was spared due to the redemption system established by the Roman empire: to release a prisoner during Passover.

The truth is, our story is the same as that of Barabbas. Like him, we were guilty of disobedience and rebellion. We were under the heavy chains of sin; we lay in uncleanness and lived in darkness. Our fate was set - condemnation to death. We were hopeless and powerless. But because of the redemption system established by a greater Kingdom (of God), we got a second chance at life. The most striking similarity with Barabbas is that the same man (Jesus) took our place, burdens, and punishment in exchange for His life. What's more, is that the life He gave us is everlasting and assured of victory over anything that could ever put us in bondage. What a marvelous exchange as a result of God loving us and not wanting to see us continue in the bondage of sin!

Reflection

- Are you taking advantage of the marvelous exchange accorded to us through Christ? Or are you continuing in the bondage of sin?
- What will you do with the second chance at life that comes through God's love?
- *My prayer is that you will choose to honor God with it.*

6

A Love That Brings True Freedom

To understand God's love, we have to go where it all began. The story of creation unfolds in what is undoubtedly the first miracle done for humanity; out of the unseen came the visible. On the sixth day of creation, we see the full circle of God's plan. God said, *"Let Us make man in our image, after our likeness; and let them have dominion over creation"* Genesis 1:26 (Modified for emphasis). All of creation was for man to exercise God's authority here on earth. God loved us; He wanted an intimate relationship with us, gave us freedom, and the power to choose.

Satan's chief goal is to deceive us into thinking that God's Love is limited. He has successfully kept away people from experiencing God's love by making them believe that being in God is limiting. Young folks think that God is about taking away their youthful fun and freedom.

However, the irony of Satan's lies is that it leads to the bondage of sin and death. When Satan, in the form of a serpent, deceived Eve in the garden of Eden, it led to a separation, a breakdown in our fellowship with God. God drove Adam and Eve out of His presence. But what can be compared to God's love? Because of His love, God had a plan to liberate man from the ultimate bondage of sin. The scripture says that God loved the world so much that He did not want anyone to perish but instead for anyone who believed in His son should not perish but have everlasting life (John 3:16).

Therefore, any moment you think about God's love, remember the true freedom it brings, and share the good news of Jesus Christ, which is the gateway to God's love of the world to enter.

Reflection

- Do you wholeheartedly believe in God's love that He expressed through the death of Jesus Christ?
- What prevents you from immersing yourself in God's love fully? Do you think that your sins are too big for his love?
- *God's love is greater than anything you will ever do. In fact, He loved you knowing what you will do, so don't hold yourself back. Fall in love with God's love for you.*

7

You Got To Love

The single most potent decision that could impact your life is deciding first to have a relationship with God, followed by relationships with others. We misinterpret love when we view it as only an emotion. When scripture defines love, it uses actionable terms like patience, kindness, humility, honor of others, forgiveness, and righteousness (1 Corinthians 13:4-8). Love is an action(s) that speaks of an internal condition.

When love is present, a walk that's not of this world is born; the walk of love. When love happened on earth, a domino effect was started: Because God loved us (the world), He gave His only begotten son (John 3:16). Because Christ loved us, He gave His only life (1 John 3:16), and when we love, we ought to give others our first place; that is, we put others first. And that's the domino effect caused by love. Love does much more than influence our relationships; it also changes our conditions and status. Because of God's love, we become His children (1 John 3:1). And when we take the walk of love, we enter into a life of abundance of every spiritual blessing accorded to us in Christ Jesus (Ephesians 1:3).

Don't feel like loving God or the people around you; instead, decide to love God and love people. Take the walk of love, not only because it looks appealing but also because it's the greatest commandment we must fulfill. Jesus' own words are clear, *"Love the Lord your God with all your heart and with all your soul and with all your mind.... Love your neighbor as yourself"* Mathew

22:37-39. Decide to love. Start with the person you met today, followed by the next person. Your life won't be the same anymore.

Reflection

- What would happen today if you decided to love the most challenging person in your life (in your family or at your workplace)?
- How will your relationship improve if you decided to be the first one to love wholeheartedly?

II

God's Grace

*"For by **grace** you have been saved through faith, and that not of yourselves; it is the gift of God, not of works, lest anyone should boast."*
Ephesians 2:8-9

*"who has saved us and called us with a holy calling, not according to our works, but according to His own purpose and **grace** which was given to us in Christ Jesus before time began."*
2 Timothy 1:9

8

Grace: The Backbone of Christianity

A young ruler went to Jesus in the hope of getting the what-to-do to be perfect and secure eternal life. Like many people today, the young ruler had accrued enough merits to be recognized as a success. From how the Bible referenced him, we know that he had been blessed and favored, making him rich. He was also perfect in keeping the law from his childhood. And, he was young, which meant that he was healthy and full of potential (Mathew 19:16-22).

We can summarize this young ruler's life this way: his past was outstanding; he had kept the law from childhood; his present life was successful; he was rich and a leader; his future was bright and full of hope; he was still young and successful. But there was one thing missing in His life - perfection and eternal life. Unfortunately, he had the wrong mindset on these two items. His question to Jesus revealed that he thought that he could attain Grace - perfection and eternal life - through self-effort or by works, like the many things he had accomplished in his life.

Because of his perspective on what he wanted, he left Jesus disappointed. Jesus told him to sell everything and give to the poor, which was basically to transfer his earthly treasure to heavenly treasure. Also, Jesus asked the young ruler to follow Him. By this, Jesus was asking him to relinquish his status and depend on Christ 100%. Jesus' statement revealed what Grace is all about: surrender and dependence. Surrendering all to Jesus, and solely relying on Him will lead to our lives' perfection and access to eternal life (Psalm 138:8).

Therefore, let Grace have its perfect work in you so that you will be perfected and receive eternal life.

Reflection

- Have you fully embraced God's Grace in your walk of faith?
- How do you know that Grace reinforces your Christian life? What evidence do you have for Grace in your personal life?

9

Grace: The Great Door-Opener

As we go through life, we often pray for open doors. We desire to get opportunities for jobs, breakthroughs in business, and success in relationships. While these doors are important, they are only a reflection of the divine door that God opened for us to have a relationship with Him. Being in a relationship with God is the greatest blessing that we will ever enjoy. In any relationship, whether personal or professional, there is always a key to the relationship. The key could be a mutual friend or a business opportunity. It is also true to our relationship with God; we need access or a door-opener. With God, this door-opener is His Grace.

The scripture states that it's by grace that we have been saved through faith (Ephesians 2:8). God's grace through Jesus opened the greatest opportunity for salvation. It allowed us to benefit from God's love and mercy. God's grace does more than opening the door for us. It teaches us. It teaches us to say no to ungodliness and worldly passions, and to live self-controlled, upright, and godly lives in this present age (Titus 2:11-12). Grace directs us in righteousness. God's grace also enables us to serve others like Stephen, who served the early church. The scripture describes him as a man full of God's grace and power; he performed great wonders and signs among the people (Act 6:8).

Therefore, as we see God's grace is the door-opener into God's family, let us then approach God's throne of grace with confidence so that we may receive mercy and find grace to help us in our time of need (Hebrews 4:16).

Reflection

- God's grace is integral in living a victorious Christian life. How do you make sure you are operating under God's grace daily?
- One major way to exercise God's grace in your life is by serving others. How committed are you to help others, especially those who are not in the body of Christ?

10

Grace: God In Action

Sometimes it might feel more comfortable to departmentalize God and the action-oriented lives that we live. We can have God in one realm where we only associate Him with spiritual things and, on the other hand, our lives, experienced in our actions and the tangible things we possess. This attitude might blind us from really seeing God in action. From creation, God has always related to us both physically and spiritually; the invisible and the visible worlds. When Adam and Eve learned they were naked, God made them clothes. When He wanted us to return to Him, He became flesh and dwelled among us (John 1:14). What made this possible? Grace did.

Grace is the entirety of God in Action. It's beyond unmerited favor. It's much more than our minds can fathom. When Jesus was born in this world, He was full of two things, grace, and truth (John 1:14). It's practically impossible to think about Jesus without appreciating God's grace.

When God wanted to express His love to us, to favor us to be in a relationship with Him, He did not only operate in the Spirit, He physically sent His only begotten Son to die for us (John 3:16). It was as though God wanted to speak to us in a language that we understood, the language of action so that He could attract our hearts to Him. When God wanted to have fellowship with humanity, He stooped down to us so that He could elevate us to His Kingdom status as sons. He raised us in Jesus Who is His Word and His Grace in action.

The most impactful way to appreciate God's grace is to realize that God expresses His attributes towards us in actions. Therefore, we need to respond with actions towards Him.

Reflection

- If you consider how your life has been, can you list things that only God's grace has enabled you to do?
- How is God's grace affecting your walk with Him? Does it lead to increased obedience and trust in God's word?

11

Grace: Speaks Of Our Worth

What's your worth? If someone asked this question, it is highly likely that we would list all the things that we have earned, starting with the most important ones. But the problem is when we view our worth based on what we have achieved, we hinder ourselves from seeing the most precious things we have. The truth is, the most important and valuable things in life are free of charge. We can never earn them; Oxygen, health, family, and our bodies are precious, yet we receive them free of charge.

Even more precious than what we see are the spiritual gifts we receive from God through Christ: Salvation, justification, hope, peace, and righteousness, to name a few. Another truth is that all spiritual gifts hint to us of our worth. It is evident in the scripture our worth comes through the blood of Jesus. God paid for our redemption from death through the blood of Jesus (Galatians 3:13-15). It's not through our effort that we earned our value, but instead through God's grace. Scripture adds, *"it's by grace that God demonstrates his own love for us in this: While we were still sinners, Christ died for us"* Romans 5:8. And when Christ appeared, grace was there to speak of our worth.

Your true worth was determined by God when He gave His son to die for you. Like how a car manufacturer decides the price of a car based on its features, we can never know our real value unless we see the value God has placed in us. It's when we see through God's grace that we can indeed access our true worth.

Reflection

- What comes to mind when you remember all the pain Christ endured on the cross to make sure your true value, as a son of God, was realized?
- How does knowing your value shape your life?

12

Grace Shaped Identity

The identity of a man is at the core of his existence. The moment anyone loses their identity they lose the meaning of life. Identity and purpose go hand in hand. It is impossible to have a purpose without knowing who you are. It means that an identity crisis initiates a purpose crisis. The first order of business for God's grace at the point of salvation is to provide us a new identification. We cease to be identified by this world and become identified with Jesus Christ and the Kingdom of heaven. Grace not only gives us a new name, but it also shapes who we are.

When we view our identity (who we are) from grace's perspective, three important things will happen. First, we will know where to stand. Whether physically, morally, or spiritually, your stand depends upon who you see yourself to be. Grace not only allows for God's favor to rest on our lives; it's the ground on which we stand because of Christ (Romans 5:2). Second, it shapes our behavior.

While it's true that our conduct could speak of our identity, God's grace shows us who we are and directs our character. We act in godly sincerity (2 Corinthians 1:12). Third, it determines who we become. Identity provides the specifications that shape our future. Grace shaped identity helps us not to hearken to our deeds but rather towards righteousness and holiness awarded by God's purpose and grace (2 Timothy 1:9).

Therefore, when we experience God's grace, who we are changed, our past goes away, and we take on the newness of Christ.

Reflection

- When you reflect on God's grace over your life, do you see yourself as a victor or a victim? Do you see yourself as more than a conqueror? How is grace shaping your identity?
- How is God's grace shaping your purpose?

13

Limitations Removed By Grace

How would it feel to live in a home with a written protocol for everything? Before doing anything, you have to consult the protocol. Without debate, living in such a home would feel like walking on eggshells and having a glass ceiling over you. Such is the feeling if you are living under the law of sin and death. Roman 6:14 says, *"For sin shall no longer be your master, because you are not under the law, but under grace."* It shows that sin had power over us and prevented us from becoming who God created us to be. Grace, on the other hand, was different.

While sin permanently limits us and hinders our lives and our relationship with God, Grace brings liberty, life and opens access to God. Under the law, we have limited power, for the law only acted as our tutor to get us to Christ, that we might be justified by faith (Galatians 3:24). Meaning we can only go so far with the law. But Paul directs us to something greater. Once we get to Jesus, we receive grace. Once in Christ, God repositions and moves us from under the law's tutoring to being under grace. While we were under sin, we were powerless. Under the law, we depended on our efforts to keep the law. But under grace, we become powerful because we no longer rely on our abilities but the unlimited power and favor of God. Grace removes all limitations to living a godly life.

Don't live a life below your capacity by operating outside of God's grace. Being under grace means you're under God's unmerited favor and blessings.

Reflection

- Do you have an area of your life in which you have not fully surrendered to God's grace?
- A critical work of God's grace is to teach us to live soberly, righteously, and godly. Soberness, righteousness, and godliness are three key indicators of Grace-dependent living. So, are these three indicators present in your life?

14

Sufficient Grace

Have you ever gone through so much in one day until you wondered where God was or questioned if He was even aware of what you were facing? Apostle Paul often faced tribulations, persecutions, and even shipwrecks for the gospel's sake. At one time, Satan tormented Paul so painfully that he referred to the experience as a thorn in the flesh. He pleaded with God to remove the thorn. But God responded to Paul's request by showing him the presence and function of grace.

It's normal to seek relief when facing hardships, but what's of greater importance is for us to remember that God is an ever-present help in the storm. His grace is present and sufficient to see us through any painful situations we face. From God's reply to Paul, *"My grace is sufficient for you: for My strength is made perfect in weakness,"* we see that God's grace is not only sufficient for us, but it also allows us to experience God's perfect strength in our weakness (2 Corinthians 12:7-10).

This grace principle is also portrayed in our salvation through Christ. While we were still sinners, God's grace appeared. We experienced God's love by Christ dying for us. God demonstrated to us the all-sufficient nature of His grace when He removed the chains of sins through the death and resurrection of Jesus Christ. And because of this, it doesn't matter what we face here on earth, we can believe that God's grace is sufficient for us, and God's strength will be perfected for us.

Therefore, it doesn't matter what you're facing today or in the future; lean on the grace of God.

Reflection:

- What situation are you facing today in which you need to focus on God's sufficient grace?
- God's strength is made perfect in our weakness. Are you calling on God's strength in your weaknesses? Do you depend on God or on your power to get you out of your weaknesses?

15

Grace In A Real World

Where Grace is lacking, bitterness abounds. Where Grace abounds, forgiveness grows. One of the coolest things a believer can do on any given day is to extend the Grace that's not from this world. The difference-maker in the true Christian life in the real world is his/her experience with God's Grace. Grace opens the door for a sinner to experience the love of God, to obtain His mercies, and to find redemption in Jesus. Unfortunately, many Christians forget that they were once in darkness, but Grace appeared. When Grace appeared for them, forgiveness showed up.

The fact is: God did not remove us from this world when we believed in Christ at salvation, but rather, Christ commissioned spreading the Good news of Grace. Christ prayed for us since He knew that we would continue in a world full of tribulations (John 17:9-26). In this real-world, God calls us to reflect Jesus and live as He did: bear with one another; love one another; forgive one another, and even wash each other's dirty feet.

We can do this only when we are willing to extend to others the grace we received through Jesus Christ, remembering that Jesus Christ freely decided to lay his life for us, to die for us. He knew that we could never be righteous by ourselves. He knew that He would need to go beyond death on the cross to include us in His life and to hide us in Him. Most importantly, Christ knew that He would continue to advocate for us before the Father. The knowledge that Christ did all this for us should enable us to extend God's

Grace to others more freely.

Are you having a hard time bearing with someone? Struggling to forgive some people or to love everyone? Remember God's Grace in your life. Remember, Jesus gave His life for sinners like you and me, then reevaluate your heart. Allow space for Grace in your real-world to experience unreal victories.

Reflection

- What makes you know that you are under God's Grace in your day-to-day living?
- How can you radiate God's Grace to the world today?

III

God's Peace

"Be anxious for nothing, but in everything by prayer and supplication, with thanksgiving, let your requests be made known to God; and the peace of God, which surpasses all understanding, will guard your hearts and minds through Christ Jesus."
Philippians 4:6-7

16

Source Of Peace

Looking ahead to what was before Him, Jesus said to His Disciples, *"Peace I leave with you, my peace I give to you; not as the world gives do I give to you. Let not your heart be troubled, neither let it be afraid"* John 14:27. Jesus knew the coming opposition, rejection, and persecution had the potential to the trouble and cause great fear in the disciples' hearts. But He also knew that the peace He was giving them was greater than what they would face. The peace Jesus was giving was based on God and not conditions and atmosphere.

What are you facing today that's causing your heart to be troubled? What is causing you to fear? Like the disciples, sometimes we are faced with things that threaten our lives, and our future seems to hang by a thread. The political atmosphere is no longer assuring, and the economic landscape has no hope. But today, in the crises we continually face in life, Jesus is still the Prince of Peace, and it does not matter what we face: When you are in Christ, you have a relationship with the source of peace.

And knowing Jesus is the source of your peace, and He is always with you, whether in the valley or on the mountains, in high waters of life, or through the fire, you will have no fear nor, its relatives, worry and anxiety. Like David, you will proclaim, *"Even when I walk through the darkest valley, I will not be afraid, for you are close beside me. Your rod and your staff protect and comfort me"* Psalm 23:4. Jesus is the source of your peace as you face life, don't be afraid.

Reflection

- What are you facing today that is causing you anxiety? Have you surrendered it to Jesus?
- Jesus is the Prince of Peace; having Him in your life means your heart will never be troubled. So, have you welcomed Jesus in your life today? If not, what are you waiting for?

17

Nature Of Peace

Some of the things we need most in the world are not easily understood by those who seek them—for example, peace.

On October 24, 1945, in San Francisco, CA, 51 powerful countries decided to come together around the table to develop an organization that will provide rules and guidelines to ensure that every nation will coexist in peace and harmony. But to this day, over 74 years later, the United Nations has never achieved the peace that was desired. What went wrong? They misunderstood peace. As believers, we must live in peace so the world can learn from us. How we live ought to demonstrate the peace of God to the world.

To have peace, you must understand peace. First, Jesus Christ is the author of peace. He gives peace based on God's grace (John 14:27). On the other hand, any other form of peace is dependent on conditions (laws), which, if broken, there will be chaos and heartaches. Second, peace rules in the heart. Paul told the Colossians to let the peace of Christ rule in their hearts. A person whose heart is governed by peace will live in peace with others. Third, true peace will guard your heart and your mind, according to Philippians 4:7. It is why those in Christ should pray instead of panicking when the world is falling apart around them.

Remembering that God has called us to peace, we should make every effort to live in harmony with everyone and be holy, for, without holiness, we will not see the Lord (Hebrews 12:14).

Reflection

- In moments of panic, it is possible to forget where to turn for peace. So, what are you doing today to prevent you from forgetting to turn to Jesus as your source of peace?
- How would you define God's peace in your own words?

18

Governed By Peace

Fear, doubt, panic, worry, anxiety, discouragement, condemnation, guilt, regret, insecurity, comparison, hopelessness, and depression. What do all these things have in common? These things can infect the heart, making it lose its power. They can make a person shrink and immobilized, preventing them from living their full life. We can call them the diseases of the heart.

We live in a world where negative news spreads like the California wildfires, leaving in its path hearts that are discouraged. Earth's foundations, which seemed stable, are now being shaken—leading the hearts of many in a state of hopelessness. Anxiety floods the hearts like a tsunami, and worries cloud our minds. But despite the darkness, the fantastic news is there is a way to guard our hearts and minds.

In his letter to the Philippian church, a church that faced persecution and false teachers, Apostle Paul wrote them saying, *"Be anxious for nothing, but in everything by prayer and supplication, with thanksgiving, let your requests be made known to God; and the peace of God, which surpasses all understanding, will guard your hearts and minds through Christ Jesus"* Philippians 4:6-7. Paul was aware that their hearts needed protection from what was going on at the time. He reminded them that when anxiety, fear, or panic arose, their hearts could only be safe in the peace of God.

On this day, when things come to threaten our hearts, we should remember it's the peace of God we need more than anything else. Isaiah 26:3 says, *"You will keep him in perfect peace, Whose mind is stayed on You, because he trusts in You."* God's peace will always guard our hearts and minds. It does not matter what you are facing; the best way to face challenges and difficulties is through prayer, supplication, and thanksgiving.

Reflection

- Considering the heart diseases listed above, which one has the highest chance to affect your heart?
- Have you found scripture references that will help you address each condition?
- According to Isaiah 26:3, it's evident that what we focus on directly impacts our hearts. Despite what is going on, is your mind focused on God?

19

Guarded By Peace

The human heart is so powerful; it shapes both our spiritual lives and the environments we inhabit. It is through the heart that we can perceive the things of the Spirit. The scripture is clear that it's the heart that rejects God or believes Christ (Psalm 14:1, Romans 10:9). It is also with the heart that we trust in God and avoid leaning on our understanding. Realizing its importance, King Solomon advised that we must guard our hearts with all diligence, for out of it springs the issues of life (Proverbs 4:23). The word of God through the Prophet Jeremiah only adds to the gravity about the heart, *"The heart is deceitful above all things, and desperately wicked; Who can know it?"* Jeremiah 17:9. Without any doubt, the heart - and its conditions - is critical to the quality of life.

So, how can we guarantee that our hearts are safe and in good health? First, we must realize and acknowledge that we all need a new heart. Like David, we can pray, *"Create in me a clean heart, O God; and renew a right spirit within me"* Psalm 51:10. And we must believe that God will take the heart of stone out of us and give us a heart of flesh. Second, we must allow the peace of God to rule in our new hearts (Colossians 3:15).

We live in a world that's full of glittery things that have the potential to change our heart's appetites. Adhering to King Solomon's advice of guarding our hearts, I believe the best way to do it (guarding the heart) is through allowing Jesus, who is the Peace of God, to reign in our hearts. And when

Jesus reigns in our hearts, God's peace will always govern how we live.

Reflection

- Do you know peace? Are you in a relationship with Jesus?
- *Without knowing Jesus, you will never know peace.*
- Are you allowing Jesus to govern all your decisions?

20

Purse Peace

How often do you stop and ask yourself, "What am I pursuing in life? Or what am I building with what God has given me?" The unfortunate truth is that most people go through life pursuing and building things that they find no pleasure in at the end of life. As believers, one of the discoveries that will bring us great joy is to realize whatever we do here on earth will have an eternal significance. Our lives have an eternal reach. So, we must continuously question ourselves: what is it that we can pursue that will go beyond this life?

One of the things that the scripture has explicitly said we must pursue is peace. On many occasions, the Word has called us to do what it takes to pursue peace. Apostle Paul said, *"If it is possible, as much as depends on you, live peaceably with all men"* and added, *"Pursue the things which make for peace and the things by which one may edify another"* Romans 12:18; 14:19. King David also wrote earlier that we should turn from evil and do good; seek peace and pursue it (Psalm 34:14). These verses make it clear that God not only desires for us to pursue peace but He also commands it.

Hebrews 12:14 highlights the importance of pursuing peace by stating, *"Pursue peace with all people, and holiness, without which no one will see the Lord."*

Therefore, remembering that pursuing peace is connected to seeing God, we should keep in mind that seeking peace stems from a desire to live in harmony with each other.

Reflection

- When you examine your relationships, how would you rank yourself: a peace-taker, peace-keeper, or peace-pursuer?
- When you disagree with people, do you focus on being right or maintaining peace?

21

Guided By Peace

As a born-again Christian, one source of joy is knowing you're a child of the Living God whose soul is redeemed. God has assured you victory despite what you face. However, being a child of God doesn't mean you won't face challenges, hardships, and disappointments. Living with no expectation of rough waters, turbulences, or bumpy roads is living with unrealistic life expectations. Therefore, the question is not whether you will face turbulence or not, but how will you navigate life's storms and turbulences without succumbing to the anxiety and worry they generate. The good news is, as a child of the Most-High-God, there is no reason to worry or be anxious when faced with turbulence since you have God's peace to guide you.

Are you facing tough decisions and wondering which direction to take? Don't worry, and don't be anxious. What you need is to welcome God's peace in your situation. In his call of the children of God to an abundant life in God, Prophet Isaiah proclaimed that we shall go out with joy and be led out with peace (Isaiah 55:12). You might be in the darkest hour, and the sea might be raging but remember that the peace of God is there to guide you; there is no way you will sink. As a matter of fact, you will be filled with praise like David, who decided he will praise the Lord at all times (Psalm 34), whether in the valleys or on the mountains.

Therefore, since the earth is the Lord's and all its fullness, seek His guiding peace in all your decisions, since those who seek Him shall not lack any good thing.

Reflection

- Is there a situation in which you are unsure of how to navigate? How will submitting it to God mean to you?
- One way to induce anxiety is to focus on what is beyond your control. Are there things out of your control that you need to allow God to be in charge of?

22

Peace Produced By The Spirit

Our natural tendency is to go out into the world to look for what should come from within us. For example, most people search for prosperity from the world while forgetting that real prosperity starts from the heart. And while trying to find God, we end up being left with the external practices of religion, missing to understand that godliness is only possible when God regenerates a new spirit within us. The truth is that when we try to achieve internal things by looking for them externally, we end up not having the peace of God, which is also an internal matter.

The scripture in Galatians 5:23 provides a list of the fruits of the Holy Spirit: Love, joy, peace, longsuffering, kindness, goodness, faithfulness, gentleness, and self-control. By their nature, that is, fruits, they are all matters that must begin from within due to the Holy Spirit in us. Among the list is peace. Unlike the world which does not know peace, we are supposed to be producers of peace.

Because the Holy Spirit is working in us, we are capable of producing and having peace for three reasons:

1. The Spirit helps us to pray in our weakness even when we don't know how we ought to pray (Romans 8:22).
2. We have the Word of Christ through which the Spirit teaches us all things (Luke 14:26).

3. We can be grateful in all things since we know that the Spirit of God works all things together for good for those who love God and who God has called according to his purpose (Romans 8:28).

Therefore, let's allow the Holy Spirit to work in us to produce peace in all situations.

Reflection

- Jesus said, *"Abide in Me, and I in you. As the branch cannot bear fruit of itself, unless it abides in the vine, neither can you, unless you abide in Me"* (John 15:4). We must realize that our stand or ground will determine whether we will produce the fruit of peace. Are you grounded and continuing in Christ daily?

23

Fruits Of Peace

If you count your blessings and name them one by one, I believe, as a believer of Christ, the peace of God will top the list. Peace is exclusively from God. Nothing on this earth can give you enduring peace, whether it be wealth, status, or government. The peace from God is not a respecter of conditions. Whether you are in a storm or your enemies have surrounded you, the peace of God can penetrate your heart and keep you peaceful.

The truth is: the world and its possessions might provide some sort of security; what they give is only external and temporary peace. The peace of God infuses the soul and the mind. It rules in our hearts, protects the heart and the mind, and directs our lives. Yet another unique feature of the peace of God is the fruits it produces.

First, it enables righteousness. Apostle Paul showed that having peace with God allows us to stand in Christ, which is being in right standing with God or righteousness, through faith Romans 5:1-3. Despite our conditions, God chose to have peace with us so that we can enjoy the hope of His Glory in Christ. Second, the peace of God produces joy in us. When we see the storm raging and unrest covering the earth, we understand that our God is with us, and all will be well. This realization of peace in the storm produces a joy that the world does not know.

Finally, the peace of God creates a future. We know that because of peace with God, no tribulation can destroy us. Our future is in God's hands.

Therefore, in whatever situation you face, invite God's peace, and things will be all right.

Reflection

- Are you allowing the peace of God to produce righteousness, and joy in your life?
- Are you letting fear, worry, and anxiety rob you of your future, or are you allowing the peace of God to shape your future?

IV

Confidence in God

"Now, this is the confidence that we have in Him, that if we ask anything according to His will, He hears us. And if we know that He hears us, whatever we ask, we know that we have the petitions that we have asked of Him."
1 John 5: 14-15

24

Because Of The Love Of God

If I asked you to use the phrase "because of the love of God," how would you use it to fill your mind and guide your actions? The phrase, "What would Jesus do?" is widely used without understanding its foundation. I believe that the phrase "Because of the love of God" is the prerequisite for "What would Jesus Do?" Therefore, it is only by understanding the love of God that we will be able to do what Jesus would in all situations.

We will have peace in all situations when we understand it's because of God's love that unto us a Child was born, unto us a Son was given; and the government will be upon His shoulder. His name will be called Wonderful, Counselor, Mighty God, Everlasting Father, Prince of Peace (Isaiah 9:6). Not only will we have the peace of God, but we will also let the peace of Christ rule in our hearts since, as members of one body, God called us to peace (Colossians 3:15). And again, the peace of God, which transcends all understanding, will guard our hearts and minds through Christ Jesus (Philippians 4:7). God's love enables us to belong to His Holy Family, where we love each other and have peace with one another because God is Love (1 John 4:7-8).

The question is, what is the effect of understanding that God loves you, and He loved you first and chose you to be His? When the foundation of our thinking and actions is out of God's love, we will be victorious.

Reflection

- What would you achieve in your Christian walk if you completely leaned on the love of God?
- The memory verse we mastered in Sunday school, John 3:16, *"For God so loved the world that He gave His only begotten Son, that whoever believes in Him should not perish but have everlasting life,"* should be the root from which our confidence through God's love is established.

25

Christ Centered Confidence

In this age when Google and YouTube have become the go-to places for answers, stakes are higher when it comes to being vigilant and staying alert against deception. During the early church, Satan, the father of all deception, depended on false teachers to deceive the church. In our present times, Satan has weaponized the internet to spread falsehood like wildfire. Why is deception so dangerous to a believer and why has it continued to plague the church since its establishment?

To realize that deception is dangerous, we must understand its effect and what is at stake. First, what is at risk is not knowing the Truth. Everything about a believer is centered on the Truth, who is Christ. Jesus identified Himself as the Truth (John 14:6), and no one can go to the Father except through the Truth of God. Second, deception affects our position in relation to the Truth. Deception has the potential to move us away from the Truth, away from the path that leads to righteousness, and places us on one that leads to death (John 10:10).

Therefore, we must recognize that deception is the number one tool that Satan will use to derail our faith.

What then do we do to overcome every deception? Since deception is only possible when we lose confidence in what we believe in, we must fortify our confidence in Christ to overcome every falsehood. Therefore, we should ask God to fill us every day with the knowledge of Christ that builds our confidence in who Christ is (the fullness of God) and who we are in Him (complete). Also, ask for spiritual wisdom and the opening of our eyes of understanding. By this, we will have Christ-centered confidence, which will protect us from all deceptions of the Devil.

Reflection

- Do you have a way to detect when you drift from Christ? Drifting is a natural process, which can happen to any believer. Having a way to know your drift is the best way to catch yourself before you move away from God's confidence.
- How do you make sure you are growing to be a confident Christian?

26

Source Of Strength

The source of your strength determines your level of confidence when facing life. If you have a high confidence level, you will go through life encouraged, hopeful, and joyful. But if it's low, then you will be discouraged, hopeless, and sorrowful. Living in a world where news channels and social media platforms feed us with continuous information that can weigh down our hearts. It is crucial to have a source of strength that increases your confidence.

Imagine you came home and found all your belongings have been stolen, your house burnt down, and your loved ones missing. What would you do? At Ziklag, David was faced with distress, destruction, and desolation (1 Samuel 30:1-6). And like how we would react, David was greatly distressed. However, David did not remain distressed for long; instead, he turned to his source of strength, God, to inquire what to do. Armed with God's response, David encouraged himself in the Lord, pursued his adversaries, and recovered all his losses.

The source of your strength influences your confidence and makes you an overcomer. David did not remain distressed by what he was facing, but instead, he found strength, encouraged himself in the Lord, and recovered all. Can we be overcomers in a world dominated by depression, anxiety, and worry? The answer is Yes, We Can! By choosing God as our source of strength like David did. From David, Psalm 119:28, we also learn that God's

Word is what strengthens our hearts. Therefore, make God and His Word the source of your strength, and your joy will be full. David reflected, *"Who is this King of glory? The Lord strong and mighty, The Lord mighty in battle"* Psalm 24:8.

Reflection

- Have you made the Lord God your strength? Does how you face your tough day, challenging situations, and uncertain seasons attest that you have made The Lord mighty in battle your strength?

27

God's Opinion

When you read about the many battles in the Bible, you will discover that the principal military tactics that set Israel apart from other nations was their close relationship with the prophets of God, from whom they inquired. Also, Israel's kings and judges' chief role in Israel was to be an ear to hear what the Lord said. This was evident, especially during wars. You will realize that any king who was successful in battle had sought the Lord before going into battle, and those who lost had failed to do so. A perfect example of one king who did not consider God's counsel was King Saul. The Bible says that Saul did not inquire of the Lord. So, the Lord put him to death and turned the kingdom over to David (1 Chronicles 10:14). His ignorance of not seeking God ruined his leadership and kingdom.

An excellent example of a king who sought the Lord was King Jehoshaphat, at least in his early rule. The Bible says that the Lord was with Jehoshaphat because he followed the ways of his father David before him. He did not consult the Baals but sought the God of his father and followed his commands rather than the practices of Israel. The Lord established the kingdom under his control, and all Judah brought gifts to Jehoshaphat so that he had great wealth and honor (2 Chronicles 17:3–6).

So, what's the take-away from this? One, people led by leaders who seek the Lord will flourish. This begins from our homes to our nation. Second, success and honor only come to those who continuously choose the ways of God in their lives. Third, inquiring from God in all matters is how to maintain a good relationship with God and follow His ways.

Reflection

- What battle are you about to be involved in, and are you considering God's opinion by seeking what He has to say? Battles could be breaking generational curses or expanding your influence through your business for God's kingdom.
- The initial step that leads to always aligning yourself with what God has to say regarding any matter is studying His word. How much time do you spend studying and storing God's word in your heart?

28

Confidence In God

When someone promises to do something for us, we are always left with two choices, to believe them or not to believe. Choosing the latter, not to believe, is easy since we don't need to look forward to anything, and there is no room for disappointments. Choosing to believe someone's promise is always not easy. To believe means we have to consider a few things. First, look at the track record of the person making the promise to determine if they are credible. Second, examine the promise to see whether it's deliverable. Since promises are an attribute of the future, these two-step processes for validating whether we believe someone's promise are vital because they determine whether we are confident about the future. The two criteria are also applicable to God's promises and confidence in Him and the future He promises.

The good news is that God has proven Himself over and over on keeping His promises. Numbers 23:19 says, *"God is not a man, that He should lie, Nor a son of man, that He should repent."* Whenever God promises, He accomplishes without fail. The quality of God that makes anyone who puts his trust in Him to have confidence is His faithfulness. Psalms 119:90 says that God's faithfulness *endures* to all generations.

Although God is always faithful, we should always be watchful not to forget what God has done for us and through us in the past. Forgetting is the biggest threat to building confidence in God. When we forget what God has done, we end up losing confidence in His Word, and we begin to depend on ourselves. It is evident that whenever Israel forgot what God had done for them, they went astray; they began to place their confidence in foreign gods.

Reflection

- Do you have a system that will help you to always remember the things that God has done in your life?
- The Lord asked the children of Israel to carry stones from the Jordan in order not to forget what He had done for them (Joshua 4).

29

Confidence Through Jesus' Provision

Imagine you're living in a small town under the oppression of a foreign power; you are considered a second-class citizen with low value. Then you meet a person who tells you to follow him. His initial encounter shows that he loves and values you. Soon, other people start following this man, and within no time, a movement that threatens the status quo in your town is born. When your relationship with him starts blossoming you find out that your friend is going to die. Not only is He going to die, but He is asking you to continue with the course of his new movement, to spread the good news.

What would you do? Where would you start?

This was real to the disciples of Jesus. They came from a region that was under Roman rule. Nobody considered them significant or valued. But when Jesus came into their lives, they turned from ordinary men to extraordinary men. Then they found out that Jesus would leave them, and they must continue with the work he began. Like ordinary people, this news saddened them. But Jesus had a plan that would assure their continued confidence. First, Jesus promised them a Helper who would dwell in them and remind them of all things (John 14:16; 26). Second, Jesus left them with His peace that would guard their hearts (John 14:27). Third, Jesus left them with His Word, which would continually sanctify them (John 17:15).

So, like the disciples, faced with the immense task of spreading the gospel, operated in confidence, we as believers and agents of the gospel need to live daily with confidence because of what Jesus has provided us: The Holy Spirit, His Peace, and His Word.

Reflection

- What would happen if you fully embraced the function of the Holy Spirit in your day-to-day life?
- How can you apply God's peace and His word today to increase your confidence?

30

Encouraged Through Faith And Love

Turn on the TV, and I bet that you will find negative news more than ninety percent of the time. We live in an era where TV corporations are continually bombarding us with information that makes our hearts sink. Nowadays, positive and good news is rare. Worse still is that there is increasing evidence that watching news causes increased anxiety and stress. So, how can we remain established and grounded in encouragement? (cutting TV time is the first step).

The early churches faced great afflictions due to their faith. Stories of Christian persecutions saturated the news; beheadings, crucifixions, and stonings made the headlines. But despite the hardship, they prevailed. The church in Thessalonians provides us with powerful insights on how to remain encouraged and deal with persecution. They were greatly persecuted but had a marvelous testimony of endurance and faithfulness (2 Thessalonians 1:3-4). Despite the hardship and persecutions, their faith flourished, and their love towards each other was evident. Through this church, we learn that the key to remaining encouraged in a challenging and hostile environment is having a growing faith and a strong love for others.

How did this church endure persecution? And, more importantly, how can we grow our faith and love for each other in our generation? The answer lies in the faith we have. Our faith should be established in God's election, strengthened by the power of the Holy Spirit, and the assurance of Christ's work on the cross. It's this kind of faith that leads us to flourish and abound in love for each other. To increase your confidence and live an encouraged life, grow your faith, and love others.

Reflection

1. To discourage you, our enemy, the devil, will always attack your faith. He will aim to seed discord between you and others. Do you have a system to keep growing your faith and love for others?
2. Of the three foundations of faith I mentioned: God's election; the Holy Spirit's power; and Christ's work on the cross, which one do you need to remind yourself continually? (Read 1 Peter 1)

31

Hiding Places

At the core of the basic human needs are security and safety. Whether consciously or unconsciously, we are continually looking for safety and security. Birds will fly into their nest during a storm, rodents will run into their burrows, while large animals hide in the forest. Nests, caves, and forests are the hiding places for animals since they only worry about their physical well-being. On the other hand, as the children of God, we face much greater danger than animals. What is threatening us is much more severe. The scripture in 1 Peter 5:8 says, *"Be sober, be vigilant; because your adversary the devil walks about like a roaring lion, seeking whom he may devour."* According to John 10:10, We know Satan plans to steal, kill, and destroy our souls.

However, despite Satan's plan, the great news is that we have a hiding place like no other. It is impenetrable by no enemy. David, a man of valor, who found hiding places in the caves as a young Shepherd, within great armies as a soldier, and behind fortified palaces as a king, couldn't find a better, more secure hiding place than in the Presence of God. He calls it the secret place of the Most-High, a shelter, and a tower of strength against the enemy (Psalm 31:20; 61:3). God's presence is where we find safety and security.

In the days we live, God's presence still provides a perfect hiding place if we choose to make it our habitation. It is an excellent resting place to find refuge against all enemies such as addiction, worry, anxiety, or lies from Satan. The LORD's name is a fortified tower; the righteous run to it and are safe (Psalms 18:10).

Reflection

- Have you found your rest in the Lord? How do you know your usual running place is in God's presence when the storms of life are raging?
- *One way to know that you're in God's presence while in a storm is through the level of joy you experience regardless of what you're facing. Read Psalm 16:11.*

32

Worry Doesn't Work

You have proven: Worry doesn't work. As you reflect on your journey so far, the many battles you have gone through, and the hardship you have faced all through the year, there is one thing you will realize: worrying is destructive. It only takes energy from you and does not add anything. Worry costs you your precious time and energy trying to take care of things that are out of your control. In hard times and uncertain seasons of life, the world defaults to worrying and depression, which leads to depending on oneself. But as believers, we are called to face the world differently.

The Knowledge that God is our provider and understanding our worth in Him will set us apart from the rest of the world when facing uncertainty. In making this point clear, Jesus pointed to birds of the air and the flowers of the fields. That, even though birds do not sow, reap, or store away in barns, God takes care of them. And, even though flowers are seasonal, God makes them more beautiful than a king in all his splendor (Mathew 6:25-30). Jesus is asking you today that if God takes care of these things, how much more can He take care of us?

We should always be very encouraged in knowing that our God, who deeply loves us and is greater than all we can ever face, is in charge, and He will take care of us. Instead of worrying about things God can handle, we should live by faith, take advantage of our position in Christ, always remembering our God is all-powerful and well-able to meet our needs.

Reflection

- What is one thing in your life that you think is too big for God? Have you considered His Love and provisions throughout your life before coming to your one thing?
- Is there an area of your life in which worry, anxiety, or fear are crippling you? Have you prayed about it? (Remember that you can move mountains through faith and prayers).

V

Walks Of Victory

"For we are His workmanship, created in Christ Jesus for good works, which God prepared beforehand that we should walk in them."
Ephesians 2:10

"Therefore you shall keep the commandments of the Lord your God, to walk in His ways and to fear Him. For the Lord, your God is bringing you into a good land."
Deuteronomy 8:6-7

33

The Ways Of God

God heard the cries and oppression of Israel and formulated a plan to deliver them out of bondage. One early morning, over six hundred men (not counting women and children) march out of Egypt and embark on a journey to freedom. But unfortunately, a trip that was supposed to take a few days ended up taking forty years, and an entire generation died in the wilderness, missing their destiny. People who had seen wonders like crossing the Red Sea on dry land and walked under God's covering ended up missing their promised inheritance. What happened?

Israel's deliverance from Egypt, their experience in the wilderness, and their entry to the promised land offers us a lot of wisdom on God's ways, fulfilling God's purpose, and walking in God's ordained destiny. What caused a whole generation not to enter Canaan and can also cause us to miss entering God's eternal glory is the same thing: not knowing God's ways.

Being like the children of Israel, being fixed on God's acts and not knowing His ways can lead us to misunderstand God and miss His plan for us. So, how do you get to know the ways of God? By having two things, a teachable spirit and humility.

God is the only one who can teach you His ways. In Psalm 27:11, David asked God to teach him His ways. This is possible when we are teachable to incline to hear what His Spirit says to us. Humility allows God to release His grace to us (James 4:6) and for Him to show us His ways (Psalm 25:9). By knowing God's ways, we avoid the most lethal disease to our destiny, a heart that goes astray from God (Hebrews 3:10). So, be teachable and humble before God today.

Reflection

- God had chosen Israel to be His people, to bring them out of captivity into their own land. But since they focused on God's act, they missed God's ways. When you look at your walk with God, how would you grade yourself when it comes to knowing God's way?

34

A Worthy Walk

The word walk is referenced numerous times throughout the Bible, from the Old to the New Testament. When the Bible mentions something multiple times, it calls for our attention. In English, walking is a simple verb that implies movement or motion. But in the Bible, it means much more. It means a way of life.

Walk is first mentioned in scripture when God was in the garden after the fall of man. God's walk (movement) led Adam and Eve to hide (separate) from God, for they had displeased Him by their disobedience (Gen 3:8). Next, we see the word walk when scripture introduces Enoch. In this scene, we see a man whose walk leads to being taken by God (drawn closer) (Gen 5:24). So, what can we take from these scenarios, where it involves walking?

We can see that our walk determines our proximity to God. With this in mind, how are we supposed to walk so that we are not separated from God but rather drawn closer to Him?

Apostle Paul in Colossians 1:9-10 provides the key to the walk that will increase our proximity to God. Paul tells the church in Colossi that their walk must be fully pleasing to God, fruitful in every good work, and causes an increase in the knowledge of God. It is the same walk we must walk today. And if we are to achieve this walk, we must add one more thing. We must know where to walk. Paul provides this insight, as well. He adds in Colossians 2:6 that we must move in Christ while rooted and built up in

Him and established in the faith per the word of God.

Therefore, choose to establish your walk in Christ, guided by the word, and you will walk triumphantly like Noah before God.

Reflection

- Do you know what else a worthy walk before God brings? God's blessing! 1 Kings 9 makes it clear that if Solomon walked uprightly, God would bless and establish him. So, are you seeking blessings in an area of your life?
- How is your walk with God in that area?

35

Your Attitude And Your Walk

Your heart's attitude will always influence how you walk with God. As your physical and mental posture affect how you respond to the world, so is your heart's posture going to affect your response to God.

Have you ever worked with a pessimistic coworker? Or have you ever dealt with a person who keeps complaining? How do you feel after working with such a person for some time? I can't be around such people for long. I believe that no one likes to always hang around negative people because they inject their negativity into our environment.

On the other hand, we all enjoy being around positive people. We know that our hope increases regardless of what we are facing when we spend time with a positive person. Both people of negative and positive attitudes can indeed affect our perspectives. But what's more important and influential is the attitude of our hearts.

It is not the people who the children of Israel came in contact with that affected their perspective on God and His plan for them, but their hearts. Their hearts' attitude made them complain and protest against God and the servant of God, Moses. Because of their attitudes, they ended up refusing to enter Canaan. Since God's plan for them was to deliver them from bondage and bring them to freedom, there was no way to go back to Egypt, so they ended up dying in the wilderness (Numbers 14).

While you are in the wilderness, you have to pay very close attention to your heart's attitude. It will affect how we view God, God's servant, and hear God's message. Regardless of what you're facing, remember your heart's attitude will determine your walk.

Reflection

- Did you ever consider that the heart has its own mind? It can influence you. Proverbs 4:23 says, *"Keep your heart with all diligence, for out of it spring the issues of life."* Given that the heart is very critical in our walk with God, what measures do you have in place to guard it?

36

Your Hearing And Your Walk

The deepest and most powerful acts of worship and being in a relationship with God are often not found in tangible and visible things. Often, we misinterpret God's direction and miss the miracles God is doing because we look for Him in the wrong places; we look for big and visible deeds to believe God. But as Elijah discovered, God does not always reveal himself through visible and loud things. As he experienced, God was neither in the wind that tore into the mountain and broke the rocks in pieces, nor was He in the earthquake nor in the fire, but God was in the still small voice (1 Kings 19:11-13).

If we are going to walk with God as Elijah did, we also must have the ability to hear the still small voice that God whispers in our hearts. To deepen our fellowship with God and walk with Him in power, we must increase our hearing focus. Until Elijah was able to remain focused and not get caught up in the power of the wind, earthquake, and fire, was he able to hear God's voice and continue his walk with God.

Jesus added weight to the importance of being able to hear when He said, *"My sheep hear my voice, and I know them, and they follow me."* To show how important hearing is, He added that He gave unto them – those who hear His voice – eternal life; and they shall never perish, neither shall any man pluck them out of His hand (John 10:27-28).

To keep operating in power and understanding the deep things of God, we must be alert to hear what the Lord is saying. Only by hearing God's voice can we walk victoriously.

Reflection

- Have you ever walked around a room in total darkness? Did you run into things such as furniture? Walking without hearing God is similar to walking in the dark. So, what do you do to make sure you are not missing God's voice?
- Do you have a way of removing distractions that might interfere with your hearing?

37

Depth And Impact

Depth and impact are directly proportional. How deep you go determines how impactful you become. For example, if you go deep in the Word of God, you will become an impactful Christian, and the deeper you go in God's love, the more you discover God's impactful grace. So, it's impossible to be impactful in this life if you live on the shallow end of life. Life in the shallow end is marked by unintentional living, false identity, and no purpose. However, God has not called us to the shallow end of his kingdom; He calls us to the deep end of His Love, wisdom, Hope of His calling, and the riches of His glory. Because if we remain in the shallow end, we become powerless Christians. So, what keeps people from going deep in God? It's the inability to see the "invisible" things of God.

To go deep where God is calling us, the first thing we need is to ask God to activate our spiritual sight to see beyond the natural realm. In Ephesians 1:15-23, Paul prayed for the enlightening of the eyes of our understanding so that we can know the hope of Christ's calling. He understood that it is impossible to go anywhere while spiritually blind. And because God is a Spirit and must be worshiped in Spirit, we must have our spiritual eyes opened to experience His deep things. Second, we also need the Holy Spirit, Who is our Helper. The Holy Spirit teaches us how to move by reminding us what Jesus said (John 14:26). And third, to follow the example of Jesus, who is the medium through which we go into the depth of God since He has taken us in Himself and He is the invisible Image of God (Col 1:15).

Reflection

- How is your spiritual sight impacting your walk with God?
- The best corrective lenses to correct any spiritual blindness is God's Word. How often do you reference the word for insight and understanding on matters?

38

God Positioning System

The use of Google Maps has become an integral part of our daily lives. It's unimaginable how we traveled a few years ago without Maps. Google has also greatly improved over time with rerouting features that help find alternate routes away from accidents or heavy traffic. However, as dependency on a current human-made system, the global positioning system, for direction has increased, there seems to be less dependency on an ancient and more intelligent system, the God Positioning System (G.P.S). Unlike Google Maps that provides only physical direction, God's navigation system provides both physical and spiritual guidance; it directs our soul and spirit through life.

    G.P.S must have three basic things to function, a transmitter, a signal, and a receiver. The transmitter is the scripture of God that transmits the truth. Apostle Paul described scripture as God-breathed and useful for teaching, rebuking, correcting, and training in righteousness, so that the servant of God may be thoroughly equipped for every good work (2 Tim 3:16-17). David called it a lamp to our feet, a light on our path (Psalm 119:105). The signal is the voice of God, which Jesus related to the relationship between sheep and the shepherd. *"My sheep hear My voice, and I know them, and they follow me"* John 10:27. And finally, the receiver is our hearts. David again shows us that it is with the heart that we seek God when he said, *"I seek you with all my heart; do not let me stray from your commands"* Psalm 119:10.

Since the word of God is unchangeable and His voice is forever true, we must make sure that our hearts are ready to receive the signal from God if we are to navigate through life successfully. To walk successfully, we must be dependent on G.P.S.

Reflection

- Life is a series of choices, moving from one destination to another. So, are you equipped with the God Positioning System? Is your heart tuned to the signal of God's voice and able to receive the transmission from His word?

39

Your Walk. Your Success

Is there a yardstick or a gauge we can use to determine our future successes? While in the desert, before entering into the promised land, Moses commanded the children of Israel, saying, *"Walk in obedience to all that the Lord your God has commanded you, so that you may live and prosper and prolong your days in the land that you will possess"* (Deut 5:33).

We see that long before they entered a land flowing with milk and honey, God had given them a means to predict their success; their walk. How they walked would determine the quality of their lives, their prosperity, and their life expectancy.

Two qualities mark a walk that leads to success, obedience to the word, and the ways of God. Obedience unlocks God's blessings. In Exodus 19:5, God reminds Israel that if they obey God and keep His covenant, they will be His special treasure from among all the people on earth. Then, walking in God's ways is how to practice obedience to God's word.

In Deuteronomy 19:9, we see a connection between success and walking. It says, *"if you carefully observe all this commandment which I command you today, to love the LORD your God, and to walk in His ways always—then you shall add three more cities for yourself, besides these three."* Walking on God's way is possible if we ask God to show us His ways. Like David, we ought to ask, *"Show me Your ways, O Lord; Teach me Your paths. Lead me in Your truth and teach me, For You are the God of my salvation; On You, I wait all the day"*

Psalm 25:4-5.

Understanding that your walk is directly proportional to success will help you lead a life of dependency on God.

Reflection

- When you look into the future, what would be the prediction of the level of your success based on your obedience to God's word?
- Deuteronomy 10:12 categorizes walking in God's way fearing, loving, and serving God, showing its importance. So, how often do you ask God to show you His ways?

40

Don't Be Distracted

When you study the book of Exodus, you will discover a unique trend. It is easy to read and look at Exodus from only the perspective of Israel exiting slavery and entering the promised land. But much of this book is about God establishing His ultimate plan for His children.

In Exodus Chapters 21-23, we see God establishing a social structure for Israel. In chapter 24, God enters a covenant with them, and from chapters 25 through 28, He shows the way of worshiping Him. But despite God directing Israel step by step, a whole generation died in transition. Only two men, Joshua and Caleb, entered the promised land. Why was this the outcome? Because they got distracted and forgot what their destination was.

Forgetting God's plan is always expensive. It often leads us to walk away from God's purpose. However, if we are keen, we can tell when we get distracted and start to drift away from God's plan.

The first sign that you're getting distracted is when you start reminiscing about your old ways or how things were before God transformed your life: Israel kept remembering their life in Egypt (Exodus 16:3). Second, when you start complaining. The moment you begin to complain about where you are, you begin to lose track of where you're going. The third sign and most dangerous sign that you're moving away from God's ways is when you start having other gods/idols (Exodus 32).

Three qualities are essential in remaining in alignment with God's plan and keeping distraction at bay:

1. Being alert and focused on God's word.
2. Remembering what God said as you make decisions.
3. Always being courageous to stand on God's word and promises.

Joshua and Caleb had these qualities, and thereby, they walked in God's rest.

Reflection

- What causes you to be most distracted from God's ways?
- What can you do daily to remember the specific instructions God has given you as you continue in your faith walk?
- Do you have a journal (online or hardcopy) that helps you document God's blessings and breakthroughs in your life?

41

Memorial Stones

In Joshua 4, we see Joshua instructing the twelve tribes of Israel to carry twelve stones from the Jordan River. He does this so that when their children would ever ask, "What do these stones mean?" They would give a testimony of how the Lord enabled them to cross the Jordan River, which was their gateway to the promised land.

Through Joshua, God introduces an essential practice we can apply in our walk with Him; setting up memorials for what the Lord has done in our lives. I think we can consider this to be the first journaling practice in history.

It is obvious the importance of the memorial stones. They did three things:

1. Acted as a constant reminder of the power of God and His presence in their lives.
2. Enabled them to remain in a state of thankfulness.
3. Helped them increase their faith and obedience to God.

Interestingly, immediately after crossing the Jordan, they faced Jericho City. I am sure the stones made it easier for them to trust God since it reminded them of what God could do.

I believe that we live when we must learn to have memorial stones that will help us in our walk with God. Documenting the thing God does for you daily is one way to create what I refer to as Jordan Journal. Having something that continually reminds you of your miracles can be useful when facing your Jericho walls. More importantly, when God instructs you to do things that may not make sense, like walking around Jericho seven times, it will be easier to believe and have faith in what God says if you never forget what God has done before. But even better is what Memorial Stones trigger (See Next Devotional).

Reflection

- The last time God asked you to do something, what was the biggest roadblock you faced?
- God is always asking us to do things that are out of our abilities, such as facing Jericho's fortified city (represents strongholds). The question is, will you believe God even when what He tells you doesn't make sense?

42

Testimony Triggers

I am convinced that God cares what stories you pass down to future generations. As you move through life, what will you tell generations to come about what God did for you? Will you have a testimony of God's favor, God's provision, and God's protection? Or, will you only talk about what did not go right and who did you wrong? What memories are you recording in your journal that will positively impact the next generation?

A testimony from a parent of what God did, shared with a son or daughter will inspire his/her heart and mind more than any gift you will ever give because it will have an eternal impact. I believe this is why, during the crossing of the Jordan river, God instructed Israel to collect twelve memorial stones from the midst of the river so that when their children would ever ask, "What do those stones mean to you?" They would give a testimony of what God did for them (Joshua 4). The rocks would be Testimony Triggers among them.

What visible or tangible items do you have that will act as a set-up for a God testimony to your future generations of how you walked with God?

You might not have stones from the Jordan, but you must have something that will trigger your children to ask about God. It could be a simple Bible verse hanging on your wall. Or a big dream that you achieved. Get something that will tell those around you what the Lord has been your Shepherd. I believe that having testimony triggers will impact your future generations and strengthen your walk with God. Whenever you look at your stones, you remember God took you through your Jordan rivers and how you walked with God in the wilderness.

Reflection

- When you look back, the last few months or years, can you list five things that you know only God made possible for you?
- Have you ever had a Jordan or Red Sea experience where you did not know the way forward? If so, do you have it written down?

VI

Growth In God

"As you, therefore, have received Christ Jesus the Lord, so walk in Him, rooted and built up in Him and established in the faith, as you have been taught, abounding in it with thanksgiving."
Colossians 2:6-8

43

Spiritual Priming

When we see great athletes winning championships, we are inclined to think that they were born great, preloaded with their skills. The truth is most athletes are ordinary people who have been perfecting their skills many years before they appeared in the limelight. They worked hard and sharpened their skills in obscurity, priming themselves for victories. They do this by strategic practice and having great coaches around them.

We can also prime ourselves for spiritual victory. Standing in Christ, we can strategically position ourselves for spiritual success. One good example to emulate is Daniel. We get mesmerized by Daniel's den of lions experience (results) and miss out on what he did long before we saw him in the den (process). So, what did Daniel do? First, Daniel conditioned his heart (Daniel 1:8). The heart is the thermostat we must set if we are to live a successful spiritual life. We do this by purposing in our hearts to live a Christ governed life (Galatians 2:20). Second, Daniel established an intimate relationship with God. Prayers were at the center of Daniel's life (Daniel 6:10). Like a runner who needs a proper diet for his body, prayers, and God's word are what nourish the spirit man for victory. Third, Daniel was excellent in his conduct. He distinguished himself among the administrators and the satraps by his exceptional qualities (Daniel 6:3). As excellent performance is the mark of a great athlete, excellence is the mark of spiritual success. Doing all things heartily and faithfully, as unto God, is how you grow in excellence

(Colossians 3:23).

So, to frequently win spiritually and grow, choose a life of priming your spiritual life.

Reflection

List three things that you are doing in the current season of your life that will help you experience spiritual victories in your coming seasons.

1._____

2._____

3._____

44

Protect The Foundation

The foundation of a building will determine its strength. Apostle Paul reminds the Ephesians (and us) they are built on a foundation in which Jesus Christ is the Cornerstone. (Ephesians 2:20). In a continually changing world, we need to constantly examine our foundation to ensure that nothing weakens our faith.

There are three major threats to a Christian's foundation. First, doctrine, which comes through false teachers. False doctrine seduces us to pull away from the truth of the cross. It makes us forget that salvation is only through the grace of God through faith. Second, unbelief. As dangerous as cancer is to the body, so is unbelief in the life of a believer. It starts quietly and small in one area of a Christian's life and spreads to affect the whole body. Unbelief makes us doubt God's love and grace. Third, fear. Fear is when we have distorted faith, that is false evidence of the present and the future. Fear causes us to start depending on our understanding when the going gets tough.

How do we protect our foundation? It is by continuing in the Word. Jesus said that whoever hears His words and does them, he will be like the wise man who built his house on the rock: and the rain descended, the floods came, and the winds blew and beat on that house; and it did not fall, for it was founded on the rock (Matthew 7:24,25). Therefore, take studying and apply God's Word seriously for your faith to grow and stay strong.

Reflection

- What are you doing to protect your foundation? Are you making sure you are receiving sound doctrine based on Jesus, keeping unbelief from your heart, and feeding your faith?

45

Indicators For Growth

At the beginning of the 2008 economic crash, many multinational and multi-billion businesses were caught unawares. Companies that looked healthy in the books did not survive the crash. Having billions of dollars in the accounts and massive operations proved to no longer be the accurate indicator of good business health. The big lesson that investors had to learn quickly was that a business was as successful as the culture that ran through the company. It was the invisible attitudes of companies that mattered. This insight of growth and organizational health could be applied in the church and in our lives today to avoid the pitfalls of gazing at the wrong growth indicators.

Through the church of Thessalonians, Apostle Paul provided us with three essential and accurate indicators for growth. He pointed to what most people wouldn't use to identify growth today, especially in the church. He didn't focus on the number of members, the amount of money, or the size of the building. But Apostle Paul pointed to the invisible matters of the heart, which are work of faith, labor of love, and patience of hope in our Lord Jesus Christ (1 Thessalonians 1:3).

So, if you are to experience growth that lasts and withstand life's challenges, you must: nurture your faith through the word of God; love people and serve others in actions and not lip-service; and finally allow your hope in Christ to produce patience. When this happens, your influence will expand as it did with the church of Thessalonians. You will be an example to many, the word of the Lord will sound forth from you, and your faith toward God will spread. You will be a tool for evangelism in our time.

Reflection

- Which of the three growth indicators shows you where you need to be more intentional about developing? Do you spend ample time studying the Word? Do you love people with the love of Christ? And are you expressing the hope you have in Christ to the world?

46

True Measure Of Faith

Spiritual growth is the accurate measure of faith in a Christian. Hebrews 11:1 says *"faith is the substance of things hoped for and evidence of things not seen."* Growth is a movement in a specified direction. Spiritual growth is the transformation (movement) to be like Christ in response to God's word: to move where God commands you.

When we have faith, we grow and do things better. It caused Abel to offer a more **excellent** sacrifice than Cain. Growth as a result of faith **elevates** our relationships. Enoch's faith enabled him to have a special relational bond with God that led God to take him alive. Growth due to faith **makes us see things differently** in our generation. Noah, being divinely warned of things not yet seen, moved with Godly fear into action. Faith grows our trust in God. Faith in God **moves us out of our comfort zones**. Abraham obeyed when God asked him to go to the place which he would receive as an inheritance (Hebrews 11).

In the church, we ought to grow. It is an environment that is favorable for growth. It is a place where we are constantly challenged to become better. And it is a place where the focus is always forward and upward. Therefore, we should be sensitive to growth and expansion seasons since we can only know that we have faith when we see growth. Corporately and individually. Be expectant of growth, and the Christian journey will be so much fun.

The three things that growth through faith will produce are excellent service to God and people, elevated relationship with God and people, and divine promotion.

Reflection

- Faith comes through the Word of God; spiritual growth comes by applying the Word of God in our lives and life's situations. In the last few months, or in the season you are in today, are you applying the Word of God in your life?

47

Guaranteed Growth

One of the most beautiful things we in the body of Christ often don't remember is the promise Christ made before going back to the Father. Jesus said, *"And I will ask the Father, and He will give you another advocate to help you and be with you forever"* John 14:16. The most important thing to remember is a believer should never live without a helper aka the Holy Spirit. Unfortunately, many believers will live without ever taking full advantage of the Holy Spirit. They fail to discover the power of the Holy Spirit that brings spiritual growth.

Here is why we must desire to be filled and operate in the power of the Holy Spirit:

1. When we receive the Holy Spirit, we receive God's raw power, and we become witnesses to Christ (Acts 1:8).
2. When we have the Advocate, the Holy Spirit, He will teach us all things and remind us of everything Christ said to us (John 14:26).
3. He is the Spirit of truth who goes out from the Father, He will testify about Christ in our hearts (John 15:26).
4. After the Holy Spirit ministers to us, we become bold, and we speak the word of God boldly.
5. Only through the Holy Spirit can we be filled with God's hope, joy, and peace (Romans 15:13).

6. God's love is poured out into our hearts through the Holy Spirit (Romans 5:5).
7. The only way to truly worship God is through the Holy Spirit: God is a Spirit, and they that worship him must worship Him in Spirit and in truth (John 4:24).

Desire the Holy Spirit to experience guaranteed growth.

Reflection

- Have you welcomed the Holy Spirit in your life? If not, what are you waiting for?

48

Breakthroughs

Being tremendous or doing great things through God in the past does not guarantee that you will always know when your next breakthrough comes around. The Bible says that Naaman was a great and honorable man in his master's sight because by him, the Lord had given victory to Syria. (2 Kings 5:1). Like Naaman, sometimes we could be successful in one area of life but still, need God's breakthrough in another area. Naaman was a mighty man of valor, but he was a leper, and only God's intervention could make him whole: he needed a breakthrough.

Naaman's story could teach us a few things about breakthroughs. First, breakthroughs come through people who might seem unimportant to us. Naaman's breakthrough came through a slave girl who might not have been very important in his eyes or the society. But she was from a place where the true God was known. Second, it's possible to stand in the way of your breakthrough. Naaman's self-importance, pride, and impatience stood between him and his healing. Because he was a great army general with a history of success and came from a land with clean rivers, he thought that the prophet Elisha would heal him according to his expectations; he almost missed his breakthrough healing. (2 Kings 5:2-14)

So, if we are to experience our breakthroughs, we must value the people around us regardless of their status since they are the channels through which our breakthroughs come. Also, we shouldn't block our breakthroughs with our expectations. Expectations of how God operates might make us not recognize the ways of God, thereby missing our breakthroughs. Are you positioned for your breakthrough?

Reflection

- What accolades or successes are potentially standing in the way of your next breakthrough and growth?
- What is your attitude when God asks you to do things that are out of your comfort zone?
- *Don't look down on the simple instructions the word of God gives you, they hold the key to your next breakthrough.*

49

Growth Through Unity

Spiritual growth is exponentially possible while in unity with other believers. If we asked Apostle Paul to summarize all his letters into a few bullet points, among the top would be, a church that remains united, grows together. Paul used the human body to illustrate to the Romans the principle of unity and how to serve in Christ's body (Romans 12:4-5). To the Corinthians, he used communication to teach them about unity. The Apostle pleaded with them to all speak the same thing, and that there should be no divisions among them, but that they be perfectly joined together in the same mind and judgment (1 Corinthians 1:10-11). While to the Galatians, he used their new identity to encourage them to cultivate unity among them. He told them that there was neither Jew nor Greek, slave nor free, male nor female, but there was oneness in Christ Jesus (Galatians 3:28).

From the few scriptures above, we can derive three essential lessons that support growth, especially among brethren:

1. Unity in the church or family rises from members understanding that each member contributes to the uniqueness of the whole and collective purpose.
2. Unity is birthed and maintained when members speak in a manner that shows that their mind is one in Christ.
3. Unity is possible when members don't allow their backgrounds to

interfere with their new identity in Christ.

To cement the above points, Paul would remind us of humility. He would tell us what he told the Philippians, *"Do nothing out of selfish ambition or vain conceit. Rather, in humility, value others above yourselves"* Philippians 2:3. Therefore, cultivate humility in your hearts so that you can have unity and grow with others.

Reflection

- What are you doing to foster unity in your local church?
- *Praying for people's needs and serving others is one practical thing you can do to boost unity in the church.*
- How do you show humility when interacting with others?

50

Completeness

To warn the early Christians at Colossi against the deception that was being spread by false teachers, Apostle Paul brought up a very critical truth that all Christians need to remember always: the completeness of man in Jesus. Other than Christianity, no other religion can definitively state that we (men and women) could be complete. All other religions are based on human philosophy, traditions, and a set of rules and regulations. Apostle Paul reminds the church of Colossi, and even us today, that anyone who teaches anything besides Christ is an agent of deception (Col 2:8).

As a believer living in the 21st century, one of the deceptions that the devil will continuously throw at you is the feeling of incompleteness. From old to young, poor to rich, many people today struggle with the need to be complete. Many have turned to following celebrities in society and looking at social media to find a sense of completeness but ended up emptier. The devil will never want you to realize that true completeness is found in Jesus Christ (Col. 2:9). If he keeps you busy trying to be completed outside of Jesus, then you will never find God. Satan's goal is to make Christians seek society's acceptance rather than God's perfect and unconditional love. Devil's desire is for you to forget the perfect work of God's grace and pursue self-righteousness. And for you to ignore the hope of God's calling for your life and have idols such as worldly riches and passions.

You will find the true and perfect completeness in Jesus. Apostle Paul summed it well, *"In Jesus dwells the fullness of God, and you are **complete** in Jesus"* Colossians 2:9-10. Therefore, finding Jesus and abiding in Him is the only way to experience completeness.

Reflection

- Have you lately considered your spiritual goals? What criteria do you use to determine your growth?
- *One way I determine my spiritual growth experience is by my sense of completeness in Christ. I have discovered that the more I know I am complete in God, the more I experience His fullness.*

VII

God's Promises

"For all the promises of God in Him are Yes, and in Him Amen, to the glory of God through us. Now He who establishes us with you in Christ and has anointed us is God, who also has sealed us and given us the Spirit in our hearts as a guarantee."
2 Corinthians 1:20-22

51

Assured Promises

"I was young, and now I am old, yet I have never seen the righteous forsaken nor their children begging bread" Psalm 37:2.

Regardless of the seasons, the fires you have gone through, the battles you have fought, and the valleys you have walked through, I believe that you can agree with David that God does not forsake His people.

Apostle Paul wrote in 2 Corinthians 1:20, *"For all the promises of God in Him are Yes, and in Him Amen, to the glory of God through us."* And in Numbers 23:19, scripture says, *"God is not a man, that He should lie, nor a son of man that He should repent. Has He said, and will He not do? Or has He spoken, and will He not make it good?"* What can we say about God's promises?

The first thing you count on is that God's promises are assured. God has tied His character to all His promises, and therefore His reputation is on the line as well. The substratum of God's promises is His faithfulness. Psalm 33:4 tells us that God's word is right (or accurate) and what God does, He does it in truth or faithfulness.

The second thing that makes God's promises assured is that a covenant guarantees them. Deuteronomy 7:9 says, *"Therefore know that the Lord your God, He is God, the faithful God who keeps covenant and mercy for a thousand generations with those who love Him and keep His commandments."* Since you believe In Jesus as the savior of your soul, you are part of the covenant; you are God's righteousness.

Because of God's character and the covenant He has with us, His promises are assured by him, and through His ability to fulfill them, they are a solid foundation to stand on.

Reflection

- What are the promises of God upon your life? Taking God's promises and personalizing them is one way to make sure you're steadfast on the walk of faith.
- What makes you doubt that God will fulfill his promises? Whatever it is, remembering God's nature, gets rid of all doubt.

52

The Best Promise

"But when the Helper comes, whom I shall send to you from the Father, the Spirit of truth who proceeds from the Father, He will testify of Me" John 15:26.

Jesus, knowing His time had come to go back to the Father, started preparing His disciples for what was coming. He knew that they would be troubled with His death and understood that the great commission would not be easy; He made them the best promise, which upgraded how they (we) related and connected with God.

Before this promise, we had no helper who would reveal God's mind as the Holy Spirit would do. The promise of the Holy Spirit meant that we would never be alone. And also, our knowledge and understanding of Jesus would continue long after the cross. In addition to having the spirit of God dwell in us, I believe that this was the best promise and gift because it also gave us power. In Acts 2, when the Holy Spirit comes as Jesus had promised, we see the timid disciples get filled with power and boldness; they begin to witness the Good news of Christ.

Even today, more than 2000 years since Jesus made the promise, our lives are transformed when we receive the Holy Spirit. Even today, with the Holy Spirit, it means that we are in continuous fellowship with God, our revelation about Christ is continually deepening, and we walk in God's power.

How can we fully benefit from this promise? Jesus provides the answer in John 14:15-17 by saying, *"If you love Me, keep My commandments. And I will pray the Father, and He will give you another Helper, that He may abide with you forever."* Love and obey Christ, and you will fully receive the Holy Spirit.

Reflection

- Do you have a relation with the Holy Spirit?
- Jesus continues to say in John 14:17, *"The Spirit of truth, whom the world cannot receive because it neither sees Him nor knows Him; but you know Him, for He dwells with you and will be in you."*

53

I Will Answer You

The most heartening thing in any relationship is knowing there will always be someone to commune with you. Communication is the glue that holds any relationship together. The promise that increases our confidence more than any other is the promise of God answering us when we call Him.

God has shown through scripture that He has an open-door policy with His people. The Lord God told Jeremiah to call to Him, and He will answer Jeremiah and show him great and mighty things, which Jeremiah had not known (Jeremiah 33.3). David testified of a time when he called upon God, and God answered; God inclined His ear to him (Psalm 17.6). Isaiah 58:9 says that we shall call, and the Lord will answer; we shall cry, and the Lord will say, *"Here I am."*

God seeks fellowship with you because He Loves you. Because He loves you, God is always ready to answer you. When we have a God, who is prepared to answer us when we call, it testifies that God is aware of the need for Him. When God says, *"Call me, and I will answer"*, it tells us that He is our beloved father. Also, it shows that He can and is willing to meet our needs.

God is not like us, who like to receive calls only when things are going well. The Lord wants us to call Him even when we are in trouble. David says that he will call upon God in the day of his trouble, and God will answer him (Psalm 86:7). God does not care who you are; He wants you to call Him. Romans 10:13 promises us, *"For whoever calls on the name of the Lord shall be saved."*

Reflection

- God has promised us that He answers us when we call Him but why don't we call God when facing obstacles in our faith walk? Could it be that we have not made it a habit of calling on God?
- *It's a promise that God will answer us, so let's practice calling him anytime. He looks forward to your call.*

54

I Will Be Your Strength

The most empowering proclamation at the beginning of any day is, *"The Lord God is my refuge and strength, a very present help in trouble. Therefore, I will not fear, even though I face the mighty storms of life."* The Sons of Korah knew that God is our refuge, and when we face the severe shaking of the earth, we only need to be still and know that the Lord is God (Psalm 46).

God's promise of strength is not similar to that given by this world. When our power comes from our material possessions, such as money, influence, titles, and positions, we are doomed to be disappointed. Anything that is of this world is temporary and can never provide us with permanent strength.

Whenever you know that your strength is from the Lord, you will do what is most challenging in the walk of faith: waiting. It is impossible to be still in the world when you are not sure of your strength. But when you know the Lord God is your strength, you will wait patiently; your soul will be at peace because you know the Lord will renew *your* strength. Like an eagle, you will fly high up above the storm; you will run the race of faith with endurance without being tired or fainting, as Isaiah said of those who wait on the Lord (Isaiah 40:31).

You will live every day declaring, *"What is impossible with me, is possible with God,"* and like David, you will boldly say, *"The Lord is my light and my salvation; Whom shall I fear? The Lord is the strength of my life; Of whom shall I be afraid?"* Psalm 27:1.

Realizing that God has promised He will be your strength will make you live boldly today.

Reflection

- What are you facing that is making you feel weary and overwhelmed? Is knowing that when you take the steps of faith God will take it with you, going to change your approach?
- *God has promised to be your strength, so activate His power in all you do by praying.*

55

I Will Be Your Provider

What is the most prominent fear or worry people deal with today? I believe that among the top fears we face, regardless of our status or class in today's world, is the fear of lack. We are always worried about a deficiency in one area or another.

If you have wealth, you worry about it not being enough. When you get a job, you worry how long it will last because the economy is not looking good. And if you have a family, you are concerned about their well-being. You worry, get anxious, and depressed because you forget that you have a God who has promised to be your provider.

Today Jesus is asking you to consider the birds of the air; they neither sow nor reap; they don't have food storage, but God takes care of them. He is also asking you to look at the lilies, how they grow. They beautify, and they're glorious than the Kings in their expensive apparel because God makes them that way.

When Jesus asks you to look at the birds and the lilies, He wants you to consider your value before God. He wants you to ask yourself, "If God feeds the birds and clothes the lilies, yet I am more valuable than they, how much more can God provide for me?"

Jesus said, *"And do not seek what you should eat or what you should drink, nor have an anxious mind. For all these things the unbelievers seek after, and your Father knows that you need these things. But seek the kingdom of God, and all these things, God shall add to you"* Luke 12:22-31.

There is, therefore, no need to worry about anything, for God is promising you He will be your provider. Just ask, and God will be your provision.

Reflection

- What is causing you stress today? Have you told God about it? Have you surrendered it to God? If God is not your provider for peace and joy, who is? Are you looking at what you don't have and missing to appreciate what God has given you?

56

I Will Be With You

The grandest lie that the Devil would like you to believe is that God will abandon you! He will make you look at your life, what you have done and been through, and wonder how a Holy God can be with you? In as much as God does not tolerate sin and evil in our lives, His love is unconditional, and He wants to be with us.

God does not want to be with you because you're good; He wants to because He is a great Father. And He knows that without Him, there is nothing of eternal significance you can do. Don't allow religion to make you feel unwanted by God. Before religion was here, God promised men like Abraham, Jacob, and Joseph, who were not of any religion, that He would be with them.

Now that Christ came and died for us, God made a spiritual provision that cements His presence together with us. Jesus said in John 14:20, *"At that day you will know that I (Jesus) am in My Father, and you in Me, and I (Jesus) in you."* In this verse, Jesus shows that it's impossible for God to not be with us if we are in Jesus.

God is not only telling you that He will be with you but also promising never to forsake you. So what are you facing today or in this season? God is telling you exactly what He said through Moses to Israel when they were about to face many battles, *"Be strong and courageous. Do not be afraid or terrified because of them (anything you face), for the LORD your God goes with you; he will never leave you nor forsake you"* Deut 31:6. When God promises He will be with you, it means you have all His attributes with you as well, thereby assuring you a victorious life.

Reflection

- God wants to be with you, but He can't do this if you don't invite Him. Sin is the great separator between God and us. How do you welcome God and overcome evil daily?
- *Connect to Jesus, the true vine. (Study John 15)*

VIII

Identity In God

"Therefore, if anyone is in Christ, he is a new creation. The old has passed away; behold, the new has come."
2 Corinthians 5:17

57

Brand R.G. – Righteousness of God

If you were a millionaire, we would most likely find you shopping in Fifth Avenue in New York, or New Bond Street in London, U.K. You would buy your clothing in high-end stores like Tom Ford of New York or wear brand names like Chanel or Gucci.

But fortunately, you don't need to be a millionaire to wear the most expensive brand name, or you don't need to go to New York, London, or Paris to shop. It does not matter your class or zip code. Your education is a non-issue when it comes to getting access to the most expensive garment. The label on this garment is R.G.

Before I tell you where to find this garment, I will tell you what will happen when you wear this brand. First, it will give you access. The phrase, "what you wear determines the doors that open to you" is true when it comes to this garment. This garment gives you access to the big G, Grace; it opens the door for you to receive God's mercy and salvation. Second, the brand provides you power/influence because it symbolizes an elevated status. Wearing this garment makes you a son and not a servant. Ask the Prodigal son who, on returning home, didn't think he deserved to be a son but a servant because of his poor choices. But the father ordered for him the best garment, which reinstated his position (Luke 15:22).

Like the prodigal son, when we come to God through Jesus, God has one garment branded as Righteousness of Christ, which gets rid of all our sins

(Romans 3:22). All we need is to believe in Christ and be baptized in Him by God's Spirit. When this happens, we become branded as God's righteousness, and our identification is changed.

Reflection

- What is your brand? When people look at you, can they see the mark R.G. for the righteousness of God?
- The brand of an item speaks of its quality and value. When you examine your life so far, have you been living on God's standards and values?

58

Your Identity And Calling

Are you aware of your life calling? The God-specific-purpose and eternal-connected mission of your life? Having a fulfilling life and successfully moving from one season to another is only possible when you're living a life connected to your calling. As a child of God, I believe that your calling and identity are linked, and it has the potential to transform lives and expand the Kingdom of God.

In Jeremiah 1:4-5, we see the direct relationship between calling and identity. It says that the word of the Lord came to Jeremiah, saying, *"Before I formed you in the womb I knew you; Before you were born I sanctified you; I ordained you a prophet to the nations."*

God first pointed out Jeremiah's identity by saying that He knew Him before He created him in the womb. The second step was for God to tell him that he was set apart for a purpose; that is, God had sanctified him before he came into this earth. Third, God told him of his assignment; to be God's messenger to the nations.

From Jeremiah's calling, we can learn a vital kingdom principle: to know our calling; we must know our identity. We have to go to God and His word to understand our true identity. Without knowing who you are, that is your identity, you will never fulfill your calling. Your identity tells three crucial things:

1. It reveals your origin and where you belong.
2. It reminds you of the source of your strength.
3. It shows the world who you are answerable to.

As a child of God and a Christ-follower, our calling and purpose is always tied to furthering God's kingdom. When you realize this truth, all excuses for not fulfilling your purpose vanish. Find your identity in Christ, and you find your calling.

Reflection

- Do you know who you are in God? Does knowing who you are trigger in you the desire to fulfill the God-appointed purpose for your life?
- What prevents you from living out your calling? (being clear with your identity is the first step to winning against any purpose blockers in life)

59

Your Identity: Your Conduct

Failure to know your true identity will lead to the inability to conduct your life in a way that fulfills your purpose. 1 Peter 1:17 says that if we are to be associated with God, that is, call on the Father, we must conduct ourselves in this life in a way that reveres God.

Before Peter gets to verse 17, he spends the preceding verses expanding on who we are in God; our identity. He starts by reminding us that we are God's elect, an election that was not accidental but something that God intentionally considered. Then he shows us that we are God's children when we say that according to God's abundant mercy, God has begotten us again to a living hope through the resurrection of Jesus Christ from the dead. Peter, who was very close to Jesus, the disciple who boldly confessed Christ's identity as the Messiah, the Son of the living God in Mathew 16:15, must have truly understood the connection between identity and conduct.

When you don't know who you are, you won't know how to behave. When you understand that your identity is in Christ, you are empowered to walk as a child of God. In calling us to be Holy, Peter reminds us that God is Holy and must be holy as God is holy.

Identity shapes our conduct because it tells us about our DNA (core makeup) and our true value. Being God's elect and children, we understand that we are born of the Spirit of God, which Jesus spoke about in John 3:5. We know that God's spirit is dwelling and working in us. Also, our identity reflects our value in God. Peter explains that we should conduct ourselves in a way that demonstrates the value of the precious blood of Jesus that redeemed us (1 Peter 1:18-19).

Reflection

- How do you identify yourself? Do you start with your spiritual identity first?
- *Beginning with our identity in Christ is how we build winning habits in all areas of our lives.*

60

Identity: Targeted

The bullseye target of the Devil in your life is your identity. He is continually aiming his destructive arrows at your essence (your identity). His chief goal is for you to lose your identity in God. He would like you to confuse your history, whom you used to be before salvation, with your current identity as a beloved and empowered child of God. Satan wants you to focus on what you have done wrong, count yourself out of God's dear family, and forsake your salvation.

According to Ephesians 1:3-6, it's not what you have done, but what Christ has already done, that makes you God accept us the Beloved. Forgetting or abandoning your identity is so vital to the Devil's success plan against a Christian. The Devil even tempted Jesus in the area of identity (Mathew 4:1-11).

When you weigh what you have done in your past, you get discouraged. When you consider what Christ has done, you get encouraged and empowered. God made Christ who had no sin to be sin for us so that we might become the righteousness of God in him (2 Corinthians 5:21). It's not what we did that cements our identity in God, but what God did.

Satan will target your identity by making you doubt what Christ did on the cross. He will make you only see things from the physical realm and prevent you from seeing things from a spiritual perspective. Satan is always targeting your identity because He understands that your identity comes with power and access to God. He knows that when he destroys our identity in Christ, we can no longer walk as a new creation in Christ by faith, believing in the complete work of Christ and relying on the ever sufficient Grace of God.

Reflection Questions

- Given the intensity of the attack by the Devil on your identity, what measure do you have in place to make sure you are safe? Jesus used the Word when Satan tempted him. So, have you stored God's Word in you to withstand the Devil as Christ did?

61

Renewed Identity. Renewed Thinking

One of the most frustrating things in the 21st century is working on a computer with outdated software. It's going to be slow, regularly frozen with the loading icon on, and most definitely, it will be prone to viruses. However, if a computer has its software outdated, we would not discard it; we would go to the App Store and do a software update.

Computers with outdated software could be synonymous with our lives. In all of us, there is a powerful software that dictates how we operate our lives. It is called the mind.

Apostle Paul's words to the Colossians in Colossians 3:2, *"Set your mind on the things above, not on the things on earth,"* show us that we could set our mind operating software (MOS) in two default settings; earthly or heavenly. This affects what we focus on, things on earth, or Christ.

Setting our minds on the ways of the earth is dangerous. Like a computer with outdated software, it leads to a life of frustration. A life that produces what God doesn't like. Things such as uncleanliness or evil desires and hurting people with anger and filthy language.

But we don't have to use outdated software; we can get an update. With a new identity comes renewed thinking. We update our software by putting on the new man who is renewed in knowledge according to God's likeness (Colossians 3:10). The new software enables us to operate in ways that please God. We live a life of love, kindness, humility, and bearing with one another.

A Christian or not, you deserve to update your software daily by renewing your mind with the Word of God, which points you to your real identity in Christ. Renewed identity, renewed MOS, renewed life in God.

Reflection

- Gauging with your habits and mental inclinations, would you say that you are past due for a MOS update?
- As long as you continue in faith, you will always need to renew your mind with the Word. With old thinking, you're slow, often stuck, and prone to viruses.

62

Designed Unique

One simple and profound truth about you that you often forget is that you are not a robot! Yes, that's right. God did not create and program you to always operate the same way throughout your life. Unfortunately, the systems we made have imprisoned us with routines and we believe that we are all the same.

Understanding that no one is like you, and no one has ever been or will ever be like you, should make us appreciate God's miraculous creative power; He intentionally made us unique. Your uniqueness originates in God, and it's that way because of your peculiar purpose.

King David described his uniqueness like this, *"You formed my inward parts, you knit me in mother's womb, I am fearfully and wonderfully made, and marvelous are Your works"* Psalm 139: 13-14. Speaking about how important we are to God, Jesus references how keen God created us. He says, *"But the very hairs of your head are all numbered. Do not fear therefore; you are of more value than many sparrows"* Luke 12:7. What are your thoughts on how God made you? Or do you allow the world to define you?

Don't allow the marvelous work God did to be watered down by a society that wants you to be like everyone else. Your uniqueness gives you a hint of your purpose!

You were designed uniquely for a reason. Your perception, your talents, and your giftedness in Christ are to accomplish as a specific purpose. So don't try to do what everyone else is doing, but every day ask God to show you what He sanctified and ordained you to do. For you will never fulfill your purpose while trying to be some else. God designed us to go through different experiences so that we can fulfill his purpose.

Reflection

- Think of your heart, spleen, liver, brain, kidneys, all your blood veins. Can you imagine that God was involved in knitting all of them together? If God invested this heavily in your creation, how much more does He want to be involved with you today? Do you let him?

63

Created For God's Work

"For we are His workmanship, created in Christ Jesus for good works, which God prepared beforehand that we should walk in them"
Ephesians 2:10.

Similar to the professional world, where people specialize in a specific trade, in God's kingdom God has a particular work that's cut out for us. However, unlike the corporate world, where you are at the mercy of others to get a job and have a career from which you will retire, God predestined work (known as a 'calling' in Kingdom terms), which He created you for and has connected it to eternity.

Apostle Paul reminds us of three truths about God's prepared work for us through the scripture above. One, God connected our ordained work to our identity; God's workmanship or masterpiece. Second, the work He wants us to do is going to be good in Christ. Third, the work will be specific since it was pre-chosen by God. These qualities of God's assignment are evident throughout the scriptures.

For Jeremiah, God tells him, *"Before I formed you in the womb, I knew you; Before you were born, I sanctified you; I ordained you a prophet to the nations"* Jeremiah 1:5. For Joseph, although his life took many detours, he understood that God was working through him to save lives (Genesis 45:7). And for

Jesus, He came to fulfill the perfect will of God.

Therefore, if you desire to do God's work, remember that God identifies you as His workmanship. When He created you, He put in you desires that will align with the work He wants you to do. Don't wait for a perfect time or to feel ready because your assignment is waiting for you. When you start pursuing your calling, God will increase your capacity to fulfill His work.

Reflection

- Have you discovered God's assignment for your life? If yes, are you doing it with excellence? If not, have you considered your identity in God?
- Not believing in who God has said you are, is the surest way to never finding God's assignment. Do you believe what God says about you?

IX

Stewardship, Relationship, & Serving

"As each one has received a gift, minister it to one another, as good stewards of the manifold grace of God. If anyone speaks, let him speak as the oracles of God. If anyone ministers, let him do it as with the ability which God supplies, that in all things God may be glorified through Jesus Christ, to whom belong the glory and the dominion forever and ever. Amen."
1 Peter 4:10-11

64

Stewardship

Poor stewardship is the number one reason families, and marriages break down and why businesses and institutions fail. Poor management of resources will cause strain and tension in marriage and family relationships. For things to be better, we must remember that man's ultimate assignment on earth is stewardship! In whatever sphere of life, you are in, God has called you to be a steward.

Stewardship is the ability to take full responsibility and safeguard what God has placed under your care. In Genesis 1:26-28 and Genesis 2:15-16, God described what stewardship is and provides the necessary elements for a steward. When God placed Adam and Eve in the garden, He asked them to tend and keep it. God blessed them with the ability to produce and multiply; anything in their domain was to flourish. God made man in His likeness to practice stewardship, not like a man but like God. But also, there was something Adam was not allowed to do. God instructed him not to eat the fruit from the tree at the center of the garden, the tree of knowledge of good and evil.

From Genesis, the story of Adam in the garden, we learn that for good stewardship to be present, two things must be in place; a God-like perspective on resources in our hands and obedience to God's instruction.

The word of God is our playbook when it comes to stewardship. When we apply what God says about resources such as money, relationships, and our bodies, we will be great stewards, and God will bless everything in our hands. We will have dominion over problems, and our productivity and fruitfulness will increase.

Therefore, in whatever capacity God has placed you today, practice good stewardship by obeying God's laws on resources, and things will be great.

Reflection

- If God would audit you like the Parable of Talents (Matthew 25:14–30), would God find you faithful in what He entrusted you?
- *The sign that you're a good steward is when you see things and people under your care flourishing. If you see otherwise, go to God's word for guidance.*

65

Serving And Stewardship

Serving and good stewardship are essential elements in living a victorious life as a Christian. When Apostle Paul described the body of Christ, he used the analogy of the body, saying, *"for just as the body is one and has many members, and all the members of the body, though many, are one body, so it is with Christ"* 1 Corinthians 12:12. He further showed that despite the many members with different functions, the body's unity is stemmed from each member functioning in rhythm to support the functioning of the whole body. As the Church is the embodiment of Christ's body, in the Church is where we should see the perfect functioning of members as members of the body of Christ.

That said, everyone in the Church has something or somewhere that he/she can serve. Far too often, when we attend church, we sit down and wait for others to serve us, thus spending many years being only consumers and not producers in the Church.

We should never allow ourselves to sit and be served or even wait for the ministers to push us to do something, but instead, we ought to be ready to serve and volunteer and add value to others in Church with what God has already given us. So, how can you serve and show good stewardship in the church?

1 Peter 4:10 says, *"As each one has received a gift, minister it to one another, as good stewards of the manifold grace of God."* In this verse, you can see the

connection between serving and stewardship. God has given us gifts and His grace; we show that we are good stewards of what He has given us through serving others in His Kingdom. When we do this, we are assured that the Body of Christ, the church, is functioning healthily.

Reflection

- Are you aware of your gifts and talents? How can you serve others with them?
- *You can know your gift by paying attention to what you feel the most weight for in your heart. Also, by asking the Holy Spirit to reveal it to you.*

66

Succeeding God's Way

We live in a world where everyone wants to be on top and first, win and take over, and be famous. And, of course, there is nothing wrong with that. It's God's desire for His children to be the head and not the tail (Deuteronomy 28:13). But unlike the worldly way, where everyone acts selfishly and believes that the only way for them to go up is by bringing others down, as followers of Christ, God wants us to operate from a different playbook if we're going to be the head, the leaders, and the successful.

In God's success manual, the theme is this; our vertical relationship must govern our horizontal relationships. What does this mean?

It means that we must first and foremost honor God. God's word has lots of scriptures that show how honoring God directly connects to His blessings. In Deuteronomy 28, Moses advised Israel that if they diligently obeyed the voice of the Lord, they would be set high above all nations, and God's blessings would be upon them and overtake them. So, as you desire to be successful, consider how much you honor God in your life by how quickly you're obedient to God's command.

Second, we must place others ahead of us. In resolving an argument among his disciples on who was great among them, Jesus educated them by saying that whoever among them wanted to be first and great had to serve others and be the least among them (Mark 10:35-45). Jesus is telling us today that the key to elevation lies in serving others, and serving others starts by valuing people in private and in public.

Therefore, to be successful, honor God in all your ways and put others before your interest. This way, you will be great in a Godly fashion.

Reflection

- In which area do you want to succeed? Have you found someone you can serve in that area and help them be successful?
- *Don't wait to be great to do something. The road to greatness, according to God's Kingdom principles, is through serving others.*

67

Serving And Succeeding

Over recent years, we have been conditioned to think that everything comes quickly, and we can negotiate the price for success. The microwave mentality, entitlement attitudes, and drive-through habits are crippling our youths. As a society, we want to get ahead quickly without sacrificing and investing in others; we want leadership positions without paying the price of building others up and standing for something worthwhile. These things have greatly affected the body of Christ.

Attending church has become a religious act, and praying has lost its heavenly splendor. We have either forgotten or ignored the principles that made men like Joseph, Moses, and Joshua, who obtained favor before God and had success before men.

For example, Joshua paid the price of success and leadership long before God appointed and commissioned him to lead Israel in Joshua 1. In Exodus 24:13, we see Joshua, as a young man, showing up early in the morning to assist Moses; he was his personal assistant in the duties of the Lord. In Exodus 17:9-10, Moses commissions Joshua to choose some men and go to battle. Joshua did not only send others, but he went to the battlefield to fight the Amalekites. And in Numbers 14:24, the Lord attests that Joshua had a different spirit, which made him follow the Lord wholeheartedly. Not surprising, only Joshua and Caleb, who had a different spirit, brought a good report from the mission field in Numbers 13.

Three lessons from Joshua's success are: Serve leaders (especially in the church), serve alongside others as Joshua did on the battlefield, and have a spirit (attitude and mindset) that will allow you to follow what God says wholeheartedly. When we apply these three keys in our lives, we realize that success in all areas begins with growing spiritually.

Reflection

- As Joshua served Moses, have you found a person to serve in your local church? Is there a way you could directly add value to the man or woman of God ministering in your church?
- How can you serve other members of your congregation?

68

Apostle's Paul Thoughts On Serving

What's holding you back from serving God wholeheartedly in the body of Christ? Is it a lack of time or a feeling of inadequacy in your skills? Do you have a desire to serve but not sure how to do it?

While it may feel like we have so many responsibilities but with less time in a day to accomplish much, I believe that there is still a lot we can do as Christians in serving others. We don't need to feel overwhelmed in giving ourselves entirely to adding value to others. We only need to develop our gifts to serve successfully and help others live a victorious life in Christ. Fellowship in the body of Christ is not a one-way exchange. It is a give and take relationship.

Apostle Paul had three primary thoughts when it comes to serving in the body of Christ. First, if we are to serve, we must be steadfast, immovable, and always abounding in the work of the Lord (1 Corinthians 15:58). Second, we must do what we do heartily, as to the Lord and not to men (Colossians 3:23). These first two thoughts are tied to the understanding that our labor will not be in vain, for there will be a reward of the inheritance in Christ Jesus. The third thought is that we have to stir up our gifts and anchor our service in what Christ gave us: the Spirit of power, love, and sound mind (2 Timothy 1 6-7).

When we keep these thoughts in mind, we will not allow fear, worry, and anxiety, to hinder us from serving God steadfastly and immovably. We will commit our concerns or responsibilities to Christ and serve others. When we live a life of serving others, we tap into God's help in living victoriously.

Reflection

- Do you want to make a difference in people's lives? Then you have to do it like Jesus: serve.
- Do you want to develop your gifts and talents? Find a way to serve others.
- *Serving others is the best way to show the work of Christ in your heart.*

69

Your Love, Treasures, And Heart

What you love and treasure and where your heart is can be used as a gauge to measure your relationship with God's Kingdom. You can use these indicators to determine the health of any relationship accurately. For example, if you are married, remember how much you intentionally expressed your love to your partner. When single people meet a prospective, their heart melts in the sight of whoever shows interest. You will observe that in any valued relationship, love is intense, the heart is sensitive, and we invest our treasures such as money and time into the relationship. It is true even when it comes to our relationship with God.

Why is looking at the link between love, treasure, and heart important in our walk of faith? Consider the following.

First, your love will determine the height of your relationship. A report given about the church of Ephesus showed that they were once diligent; they had persevered and had endured hardships for the name of Jesus. But there was a problem; they had grown weary. Why? Because they had forsaken their first love, which had caused them to fall (Revelation 2:1-5).

Second, your treasure shows where your heart is (Mathew 6:21). Your treasure is what you value. If it is your time, where do you spend the most time? If it's relationships, which relationship do you consider indispensable? And if it's money, where do you spend most of your money?

Third, it is from your heart where you connect and relate with God. It should be pure and guarded, for from it flow the issues of life (Proverbs 4:23). So by considering your love, treasures, and your heart, you can tell how close you are to God. For you to live a victorious life, your first love should be God, your treasures should be in heaven, and your heart must be where Jesus abides.

Reflection

- When you consider what moves you, what makes you shed tears, and what makes you sing with joy, would you say that your life reflects God's kingdom? Are your passions connected to Christ?

70

Sacrifice, Commitment, And Value

"Actions speak louder than words" has become a universally accepted truth. This is because actions carry more weight and involve more energy. In the kingdom of God, we would say, sacrifice speaks louder than words. Throughout the Bible, there is an important kingdom principle that Satan would never want you to learn. The principle states, your sacrifice is directly proportional to the value you see and is an indicator of your level of commitment.

The sacrifices of Abel and Cain in Genesis 4:1-15 is the first time we see this principle. Based on the sacrifices they brought to God, we can see who was committed and, most important, who placed a higher value on God.

God applied this principle when redeeming us, and He expects us to use it too. When God created us, He placed the highest value on us, in that He created us in His image and likeness. It was because of the value He had on us that enabled Him to make the greatest sacrifice to return to Him. John 3:16 and Romans 5:8 clearly show that it was the love (value) of God on us that Christ died (sacrificed) for us.

God's great sacrifice and the highest value on us gave room to His most profound commitment to us. Philippians 1:6, Colossians 1:22, Jude 1:24, and Ephesians 1:4 all show the commitment in Christ that God has for us, to be holy and blameless. The sacrifice principle plays out from Genesis to Revelation. What's even more profound is that if we grasp this principle, we will elevate our worship.

The connection: What is the primary indicator that God loves you? The sacrifice of His Son on the cross. How do we respond to this love? By offering our bodies as a living sacrifice (Romans 12:1).

Reflection

- Looking at your time, one of the most precious resources we have, where and how you spend it, what can it tell about your values and commitment?
- Would you consider that you responded to God's gift of Jesus Christ in a manner that shows you appreciate what God did?

X

Victorious Warfare

"For the weapons of our warfare are not carnal but mighty in God for pulling down strongholds, casting down arguments and every high thing that exalts itself against the knowledge of God, bringing every thought into captivity to the obedience of Christ."
2 Corinthians 10:4-5

71

Understanding Warfare

In the general elections, a central question the American presidential candidates get grilled on is how they will handle military spending. How a nation budgets and spends on its military will determine the size of military personnel and the kind or types of weapon they will have, which determines the strength of the whole nation. Therefore, questions on military spending uncover a candidate's understanding of warfare dynamics and their battle-ready strategies.

Being part of God's kingdom, Apostle Paul did not want us to be ignorant of the warfare we face as believers. Therefore, he wants us to understand the following: First, to win a battle, we must be on the right battlefield. Paul reminded us that our warfare is not in the flesh but the heavenly realm, which is the spiritual battlefield. Second, we must know our enemy. Our enemies are principalities, powers, and the rulers of the darkness of this world (Ephesians 6:12). Third, to defeat the enemy, we must have and know how to use the right weapons. Our weapons are mighty through God to the pulling down of strongholds; Casting down imaginations, and every high thing that exalts itself against the knowledge of God and bringing into captivity every thought to the obedience of Christ (2 Corinthians 10:3-6).

Victorious living calls on you to understand how to wage spiritual battles. Failure to realize that your battles are not against flesh and blood (things that affect your physical and emotional beings), you will be a defeated Christian.

To fully fit yourself with the Heavenly armory, use the battlefield manual of the Word of God.

So, whatever battles you're facing today, understand that choosing the right battlefield, using the correct weapons, and knowing the real enemy is how we become battle-ready and conquerors.

Reflection

- How do you deal with things that cause you stress? Do you pray about them or complain? Do you surrender your concerns to God, or do you carry an unnecessarily heavy load in your heart?
- One sign to know that you're giving in to the enemy is when you notice fear filling your heart.

72

Underlying Principles

Are there books in the Bible that you don't frequently read? There are some books in the Bible if you look on the surface, you might think they are obsolete and not applicable to today's living. Leviticus is one of those books that can easily fall in this category.

However, after you read the first few chapters of Leviticus, the thought of the sacrifice of Christ on the cross may have crossed your mind. It is full of ordinances of God's requirement for Jewish sacrifices to God and how they approached the altar. But with God's revelation, you won't get caught up with the Jewish practices at the time; instead, you will capture the underlying principles of offerings and approaching God.

In this book, God teaches the children of Israel how to offer sacrifices that are acceptable to Him and the requisite mannerism at the altar.

Indeed, we do not offer animal sacrifices as the children of Israel were instructed to do. And we might not be offering grain offerings, fellowship offerings, and sin offerings as they did, but that does not negate us from learning and applying the fundamental principles of offering to God.

With the perfect example of Jesus Christ, who is a bridge to the old testament, He freely Gave the perfect sacrifice by becoming sin so that in Him, we might become the righteousness of God (2 Corinthians 5:21; John 10:17–18). We must learn to give our offering out of our own free will, it must be without blemish (holy), and, most importantly, we should always pray and desire that our offering will be a good aroma to the Lord. Lastly, we must learn how to honor those who work at the altar, the servants of God. Always read the Word of God with the awareness of the underlying principles.

Reflection

- How do you best read the word of God for full understanding?
- *As I study the Word of God, I have realized that if I fail to invite the Holy Spirit to reveal the scriptures, I never fully understand God's word.*

73

Apply First-principles Strategy

Do you know how much information you receive on a single day? The equivalent amount of 34 gigabytes of information per day, a quantity to overload a laptop within a week. With this high volume of information, we are at an increased risk of deception and a great need to know how to siphon the right information to live Godly lives.

In Physics, there is a concept known as the first-principles. It means the self-evident idea or a fact that we cannot deduce from any proposition or broken down from any other. Otherwise stated, it's breaking information to its basics. We can apply first-principles thinking in understanding the word of God and using it in our lives.

Apostle Paul used the first-principles approach to spread the gospel. To make sure the gospel was understood and received, he broke down his message, through the power of the Holy Spirit, to the elementary concepts such as faith, belief, grace, etc. One good illustration of this approach was when Paul explained to the Christians in Rome about God's love and provision. To convince them and us that the love of God is sure; nothing could separate them/us from this love, he reminded them/us the demonstration of God's love by saying, *"He who did not spare His own Son, but gave Him up for us all—how will He not also, along with Him, graciously give us all things?"* Romans 8:31-39. With this use of first-principle, Paul removes any doubt that could linger in us about God's love and provision.

So, what are you facing today? What answers do you need? The way to go about it in any situation you're facing is by determining the first-principle about your situation through God's word. You will be more than a conqueror when you understand the fundamental truth of God's word and apply it in your life.

Reflection

- How do you differentiate between good information and the right information?
- *Far too often, we think that because something sounds good, it's right. When it comes to defeating the Devil, the father of deception, we must learn to apply first-principles thinking to know what is right before God.*

74

God's Strategy

Your strategy or God's strategy; which one do you depend on for victorious living? God's plan for the children of Israel was simple and straightforward: to go up and possess the land that the Lord had promised their fathers. They were not to be afraid or be discouraged. But when it came time to take their promise, the children of God came up with their own strategy; they chose first to send men to spy the land, to go before them, which indeed was a good military strategy, but was it? (Deuteronomy 1:21-24).

What is the effect of abandoning God's plan and strategy for our lives?

As we can learn from the children of Israel, when we desert God's plan and strategy for our next move in life, the first thing that happens is we will have a distorted perspective of what God has done for us this far. The Israelites thought God hated them, therefore removing them from Egypt only to die in the Amorites' hands. Second, we will be discouraged about the future where God is taking us. Israel saw the people in their future to be greater and mightier than they were, appearing to them as grasshoppers. Third and most important, it will lead to rebellion and rejection of God's destiny for us. Grabbed by fear of the inhabitants of Canaan, Israel rebelled against God's command and refused to enter into the promised land.

What must we do? Despite where we are, we must first have faith in God and trust His promises; to bring us to an expected or desired end (Jeremiah 29:1-11). Second, we must put our hope in God alone (Psalm 33:20-22).

Third, we must have the courage to choose to obey God's voice (Numbers 13:30-14:9). By doing this, we can rely on God's strategy.

Reflection

- When facing a fork on the road to your destiny, do you lean on your strategy or God's plan?
- How do you know that you're fully trusting God in all your decisions?
- *Don't allow a grasshopper mentality to halt you from entering God's rest as Israel did.*

75

The Word of God

We live in the information age. It has been made easy to access information from anywhere and anytime on the planet. Nowadays, it requires no specialized training to find information or even do many things that need specialists. Google, Siri, and Alexa are the go-to-places for any info.

You can find information to fix your car, cell phone, make home improvements, and a happy family online. But there is one major issue that our information age lacks; the truth, insight, and revelation of building a victorious life in God. The misconception that has crippled the world and the church today is that information is power. Whereas truth, insight, and revelation, which you can only find in God's Word, is what activates the real power that enables permanent change.

God's Word provides what the information age can't and has qualities that neither Google, Siri, nor Alexa has. First, the Word of God is alive and active. Hebrews 4:12 says that God's Word is *"sharper than any double-edged sword; it penetrates even to dividing soul and spirit, joints, and marrow; it judges the thoughts and attitudes of the heart."* It means God's Word can see the heart's intent and bring to light what darkness tries to cover. Second, the Word of God is truth and has the sanctification power from sin. Jesus' prayer in John 17:17 is that God will set us apart by His Word. And third, the Word of God gives life to our spirit (John 6:63).

God's Word provides the most accurate counsel in living victoriously in the present age because of its attributes. It is never outdated nor does it require revision. Therefore, if you want to continue to operate in power, have a spiritual advantage, and be successful, wage war and win, you have to rely on the counsel of God's Word.

Reflection

- How often do you run to God's Word for reference before making important life decisions?
- When God gives counsel through His Word, how quickly do you follow through?
- *The best way to never go astray is by hiding God's Word in your heart (Psalm 119:11).*

76

Godly Counsel

Have you ever tried or seen someone try to assemble a piece of house furniture such as a TV stand without using the manual? My experience of not using a manual while putting together furniture was not great. I always have to redo the work after seeing that the furniture is not stable because I missed a few screws.

Interestingly, the manufacturer always includes the manuals in the enclosure that comes with the furniture, and it is the first thing we pull out from the box, but we put it aside as though not necessary. If you think you have never done this before, reflect again.

The idea of the manufacturer's manual isn't a modern thing, and it did not even originate with us; it was God's thing since the foundation of the earth. We can trace it back to the book of Genesis when God provided Adam with the instructions on how to function here on earth.

Like how when you ignore a furniture's manual can lead to things breaking, the moment we don't seek God's counsel in any decision, we violate God's manual for conducting our affairs, which comes with a cost attached to it.

A good example is Joshua's case in Joshua 9:14 when Israel entered into a treaty with the Gibeonites without asking God's counsel. They ended up being in a costly relationship, affecting them until King David's time (2 Samuel 21:1). When Adam did not abide by God's counsel, sin and death dominated humanity up to today.

God's counsel is the bloodline of living a victorious life. When you seek to hear what the Lord has to say in any situation, you will find success. Proverbs 19:20 promises that when we listen and receive Godly counsel, we will be wise.

Reflection

- How often do you seek God's counsel in matters you face?
- Do you know the best strategy for winning battles in your life?
- *"For by wise counsel you will wage your own war, And in a multitude of counselors, there is safety" Proverbs 24:6.*

77

A Name With Authority

Jesus! The name above all other names—the name with authority and full of power. More than 2000 years after heaven announced it, it's still the principal authority in heaven and earth. God highly exalted His Son and bestowed on him this name – Jesus, so that under its authority, every knee should bow, in heaven and on earth and under the earth, and every tongue confess that Jesus Christ is Lord, to the glory of God the Father (Philippians 2:9-11). In this name, God has called us, established, and from it, we are to exercise God's authority in our personal lives.

The greatest joy for us, believers, is knowing that we have access to God because of the name of Jesus. We know that by Him we have; a way to the Father, the truth about the Father, and life from the Father (John 14:6). Living in a time where hope is scarce, we can be the beacon of hope because we know Jesus. Because of Christ and the hope of His calling, we must be visible in this world because we have the light of God, who is Jesus. When we radiate Christ, who is the radiance of God's glory (Hebrews 1:3), we bring light into the world and lives of those who walk in darkness (Matthew 5:14-16).

The issue is not the hopelessness or the darkness that seems to envelop the world; the problem is we are not applying the authority that we have in the name of Jesus! Let's remember that we are permitted to use the name of Jesus in our lives and the world around us. As Jesus said, *"And whatever you ask in My name, that I will do, that the Father may be glorified in the Son"* John 14:13. Your victory depends on Jesus' name.

Reflection

- How regularly do you call on the name of Jesus? The world has made cursing a regular thing, and the name of Jesus a taboo. That's not right.
- How do you make the light of Christ shine through your life? Is your life reflecting Jesus?

78

God's Presence Your Fortress

Being a king from a tender age and a great warrior who led a mighty military to many victories, David was well-versed in military strategies and tactics. One piece of advice to winning battles David would share with us is always to have a strong fortress. After consolidating power as a new king, the scripture says, *"David dwelt in the fortress, and called it the city of David. He built it up all the way around from the supporting terraces inward"* 2 Samuel 5:9. I believe David wouldn't only tell us that fortresses are essential as a military strategy, but he would go further to say that they are crucial for spiritual victories.

David declared that *"The Lord is my rock and my fortress and my deliverer, my God, my rock, in whom I take refuge; My shield and the horn of my salvation, my stronghold"* Psalm 18.2. Like him, especially in the time we live in, we must make the Lord our fortress. Our Heavenly Father as a fortress is strong and mighty in battle (Psalm 24:8). His word stands and is firmly fixed forever in heaven (Psalm 119:89), and He has promised to strengthen us and help us and to uphold us with His righteous right hand (Isaiah 41:10).

As the earth's foundations are being shaken, hopelessness and fear fill people's hearts, and distress is evident everywhere. we must make God our fortress and stronghold. We must always run to God - put our trust in Him, live a life of full dependency on Him, and be like Mount Zion, which cannot be shaken but endures forever. And our hearts will be filled with hope, and no distress will overcome us.

Definition: A fortress is a stronghold that serves as a command post or a resourcing center.

When it comes to spiritual matters, God is our must go-to-place for instructions and replenishment.

Reflection

- Have you made God your fortress today?
- Is there an issue you need to be in God's presence to ask for a winning strategy?
- *God is in the business of making our burdens light because He loves us.*

79

Safety In The Secret Place

Psalm 15:1 says, *"LORD, who may abide in Your tabernacle? Who may dwell in Your holy hill?"* What an important and powerful question David asked here! The same question that we should be asking ourselves today. As David asked, in our walk of faith we must also ask, *"Who can remain in God's presence?"*

The rest of Psalm 15 Provides a practical and straightforward answer. David writes in verse 2, *"He who walks uprightly, works righteousness, and speaks the truth in his heart."* David's love for the house or presence of God is evident across the many Spirit-inspired psalms he wrote. He wrote, *"I was glad when they said to me, 'Let us go into the house of the LORD'"* Psalm 122:1. What did David understand about dwelling in the secret place of God?

David understood that there was a great benefit of abiding (being and continuing) in God's presence. He wrote in Psalm 91, *"He who dwells in the secret place of the Most High shall abide under the shadow of the Almighty."* Indeed, He shall deliver you from the snare of the fowler and from the perilous pestilence. He shall cover you with His feathers, under His wings, you shall take refuge; His truth shall be your shield and buckler."* Otherwise stated, in the presence of God, there is safety.

It doesn't matter what you are going through or what danger seems imminent; in God's presence is where you will always find safety. So, to live a victorious life, it's critical to free up your mind from the worry and concerns of destruction and tyranny that ungodly people suffer by walking uprightly, standing in Christ's righteousness, and having the truth in your heart. Safety in God's presence is the key to living a fear-free life.

Reflection

- What is your relationship with God's presence? Is it a place you reside in, or you only visit on Sundays?
- Have you fully surrendered all your worries and concerns about your safety, especially your soul, in God's care?

80

Danger To Your Calling

Your victorious life is largely dependent on your calling. While your gifts and talents are what God gave you, your calling is where God has called you to use your gifts and talents; it's your divine-purpose and Kingdom-mission. Your calling, like your gifts and talents, is connected to living the life God created for you. With its importance, it means that the enemy who is always working to prevent us from enjoying our best life will work to undermine our calling. He will set up an opportunity for you to self-sabotage your calling. So, what are the most significant dangers to your calling?

King Saul, the first King of Israel, is the best example to give us a panoramic view of the dangers to our calling. But before his calling was in jeopardy, what was unique about Saul? First, God chose him as commander over God's inheritance. The prophet Samuel made it clear that Saul's kingship was not about him, but rather about God's people. Second, Saul was transformed by God's spirit into a new man who could prophesy. Third, when Samuel presented him to the people, he immediately got favor before them (1 Samuel 10).

King Soul's end was not the same as his beginning. Why? God rejects Saul, the Spirit of God leaves him, and he dies in his enemies' hands (1 Samuel 15). What went wrong?

Saul's disobedience to God's word through the prophet and the fear of people was what destroyed his calling. Disobedience and fear of men are still the two most significant threats to our calling today. They prevented Saul from fulfilling his calling and upended his Kingdom-mission.

So, choose always to be obedient to God's Word, for it is the guide to our calling and never fear people for they can derail you from your Kingdom-mission.

Reflection

- Are you aware of your God-calling for your life?
- Are you making sure that you're safe from the two big threats to your calling by obeying God even in small tasks?
- *Always remember that nothing is too small or insignificant to obey God in your life.*

81

Vision, Patience And Trust

God said, *"For the vision is yet for an appointed time, but at the end, it shall speak, and not lie: though it tarries, wait for it; because it will surely come, it will not tarry"* Habakkuk 2:3. It is impossible to live victorious without fulfilling God's vision for your lives.

When you have a vision, remember that it's not on your terms but God's; you don't set the time for it to pass, but God does; you can't use your means to accomplish the vision. You are simply partakers of God's plan, and He allows you to have a foresight of what He is going to do.

Realizing that your vision is from God, He has revealed it to you, you will see the need to align all your life with His grand plans for the vision to pass. You will no longer walk by sight but by faith. And you will discover that your best ally when you receive God's revelation is patience. Since with patience, you will wait upon the Lord to perform His word, to bring to pass what He has shown you.

But patience is possible when we align our expectations with God's word, surrender every situation to Him through prayer, and be grateful at all times (Philippians 4:6), thereby developing trust in God to wait on Him.

The advantage of trusting in God is that you become immovable like mount Zion, which cannot be shaken but endures forever (Psalm 125:1). He renews your strength like that of an eagle; you won't get weary until the vision comes to pass (Isaiah 40:31).

Thus, as the Lord spoke through Habakkuk, you are assured that God's vision in your lives will come to pass regardless of time. Have patience and trust in God; He is watching to perform His word.

Reflection

- Do you have your God-given vision written down? Habakkuk 2:2 instructs us to write down our visions; to make them visible.
- What does the word of God say concerning the vision you have?
- *Finding scriptural references for your vision is the best practice for growing your patience and trust in God.*

XI

Satisfying and Fulfilling Life

"The Lord is my shepherd; I shall not want.
He makes me lie down in green pastures.
He leads me beside still waters.
He restores my soul.
He leads me in paths of righteousness
for his name's sake."
Psalm 23:1-3

82

Reflecting On God's Goodness

One way of staying encouraged and filled with praise is through reflecting on God's goodness. Reflecting on how far you have come as a Christian is far beyond remembering events. It is looking back and seeing God at work: realizing that His hand of provision and protection was upon you; knowing that His sufficient grace, renewed-every-day mercy, and unconditional love was ever-present.

Whatever season you are in today, it's imperative to pause, look back, and reflect on the goodness of God. You do this to celebrate and glorify God, knowing that were it not for Him being on your side, you wouldn't have made it this far.

The major thing that reflection produces is a grateful heart. Upon establishing his Kingdom, defeating Israel's enemies, and bringing the Ark of the covenant in Jerusalem, King David delivered a psalm of thanksgiving (1 Chronicles 16:7-36), which was full of reflection. David calls his people to give thanks to the Lord; to call upon His name; to make known God's deeds. He referred to the works of God wondrous; the Lord great and greatly to be praised; and ordered that God, who had watched them through and kept His covenant for generations to be feared (honored) above all gods. He ended by saying, *"Oh, give thanks to the Lord for He is good! For His mercy endures forever."*

When you reflect on God's goodness, the favor He has bestowed on you, and His love for you, what song will you sing? Will it be of praise like David? I pray, may you glorify God with thanksgiving as you move from one season to another; may you fill your mouth with His praise as this is the way to live a fulfilling life.

Reflection

- How do you keep track of God's blessings in your life?
- The fastest way to move from a bad day to the worst day is by forgetting what God has done in your past. In contrast, the easiest way to move from the worst day to a great day is by reflecting on God's goodness in your life.

83

No Wasted Experiences

Moses said to the children of Israel, *"Remember how the Lord your God led you all the way... to humble and test you to know what was in your heart... He humbled you, causing you to hunger, and then fed you with manna, which neither you nor your ancestors had known, to teach you that man does not live on bread alone but on every word that comes from the mouth of the Lord"* Deuteronomy 8:2-3.

What the Israelites could have seen as only a painful journey through the hot desert to get to the promised land was filled with experiences that at the time would have looked meaningless. The exodus story of Israel's children has a remarkable resemblance to our lives and journey of faith. God takes us through experiences that are knit with lessons.

I believe God intentionally allows us to go through things that make us know God more. They create more dependency on Him and the realization that He is a living God.

Whether you went through – or are still going through – the desert, like the children of Israel, lying in green pastures and walking beside quiet waters, or you are in the darkest valley, after the experience, I am sure that you will attest that God used your journey for something greater.

It might be the testing of your heart that God wanted to do or to teach you something new as He did with Israel's desert experience. Whatever it is, God's experience doesn't go to waste. They are the seed for a deeper revelation of His plans. They condition our hearts to trust Him fully and walk with Him mightily. Growth in faith is only possible when you learn from the experiences God put you through.

Reflection

- When you examine your walk with God, would you say that you take the time to learn what God is teaching you? or do you, like the children of Israel, complain about what is happening outside and miss to see what God is doing in you?
- *Complaining robs all value from the experiences God puts us through.*

84

Gratitude: An Attitude Changer

The fastest way to start living a fulfilling and satisfying life is when we begin to express gratitude. In a world where material things seem to matter most, it is easy to move through life focused on accumulating things that don't matter much and ignoring what's really important.

Looking at what we don't have, makes us fail to recognize what God has freely given us. When this happens, it seeds unhappy and joyless living. But when you live a life of thanksgiving, it leads to a joyful and satisfying life.

To live a life of gratitude, then we must know three things. First, thanksgiving originates from the heart, from within, and not from outside: From seeing God's invisible spiritual work, we still thank God for the yet manifested spiritual-physical works of God. This way, we sing the hymn of faith in Habakkuk 3:17-18.

Second, true thanksgiving causes generosity. Apostle Paul prayed that the Corinthians would be enriched in every way to be generous on every occasion, and their generosity would result in thanksgiving to God (2 Corinthians 9:11).

Third, thanksgiving eradicates anxiety. Apostle Paul points out a critical piece to prayer when he wrote to the Philippians. He told them that they should be anxious for nothing, but in everything by prayer and supplication with thanksgiving, they should let their request be known to God (Philippians 4:6). This is still applicable today. We eliminate worries of this life not by the possessions we have but through prayer with thanksgiving.

I pray that you will focus on God, your spiritual position in Christ, and all the spiritual blessings today. May you sing this Song from Habakkuk 3:17-18.

"Though the fig tree may not blossom, nor fruit be on the vines;
Though the labor of the olive may fail, And the fields yield no food;
Though the flock may be cut off from the fold, and there be no herd in the stalls.
Yet I will rejoice in the Lord; I will joy in the God of my salvation.
Amen."

Reflection

- What have you done to deserve your life?

85

Humility: Promote Unity And Blessings

What is your attitude when someone asks to change? When you are asked to do things What is your attitude when someone asks to change? When are you asked to do things differently from what you have always done? Change is what God uses to make us learn to trust him more, break old habits, and strengthen believers' bond of unity.

A church led by the Holy Spirit must always be ready to go through changes united. Without unity, a church will be like the early church of Corinth, which concerned Apostle Paul. It was enriched in everything by God in all utterance and knowledge and a good testimony, but there were divisions among them (1 Corinthians 1:1-12).

How does a church grow in unity? How does home stand together? How can you foster unity among people you interact with as a believer? The answer is humility. Jesus chose to remain humble as he came down from His kingship to be our savior to unite us with God.

"Christ, being in the form of God, did not consider it robbery to be equal with God, but made Himself of no reputation, taking the form of a bondservant, and coming in the likeness of men. And being found in appearance as a man, He humbled Himself and became obedient to the point of death, even the death of the cross" Philippians 2:6-9.

Humility is the key to growing with others. Where there is humility, pride can't exist. Humility shapes your attitude to the point of God, giving you more grace. James 4:6 says, *"God resists the proud, but gives grace to the humble."*

So, remember, humility is not only important in uniting us with others but also in enabling us to experience unity with God and receive his grace and blessings. Where there is unity, blessings abound (Psalm 133:1-3).

Reflection

- We lose humility when we forget that it was one of Christ's pillar attributes. At times, we think that being humble is a weakness, whereas it is an attribute of men like Jesus. Remember the last time someone corrected you; how did you respond? What did it say about humility in you?

86

Seeing Value in Others

"The Spirit of God, who raised Jesus from the dead, lives in you. And just as God raised Christ Jesus from the dead, He will give life to your mortal bodies by this same Spirit living within you." These are the words of Paul in Romans 8:11.

Paul, an apostle to the Gentiles, often dealt with issues in the early church that were predominantly full of Gentile converts. Given Paul's background as a Jew, it would have been difficult for him to find common ground with people who worshiped other gods. But his words indicated that he saw beyond the surface of how people looked, behaved, or worshiped. His earlier conversion to Christianity must be what helped him have a more profound revelation of Christ and see Christ in people as he wrote Romans.

His ability to see God in others led to his passion for people. His letters are full of evidence of how he esteemed the brethren: he prayed for them and wanted them to grow in faith. Whenever we look beyond what makes us different, we start to see the Spirit of God in us; we see the Spirit of God at work in others. Instead of looking down on people, we look up in thanksgiving and prayer for others. Prayer is a powerful gift that we can offer anyone. Unlike material gifts that don't add any eternal value and their effects are only superficial, prayer calls God's blessings to whoever we pray for, and its impact is life-transforming.

So, whenever you meet a believer or even a nonbeliever, be utterly mindful of the power of God that works in them or can work in them to be who God wants them to be. By doing this, you will value, love, and honor others, a recipe for a fulfilling life.

Reflection

- People are the most influential environmental factors that affect how fulfilled we live. However, it's not how they behave that makes a difference; it's how we see them. So, how do you see people? Do you see their weakness, or do you see the power of God?

87

God Dependency - Trust

I believe the biggest threat to victorious living is fear and its derivatives worry, anxiety, and depression. The Anxiety and Depression Association of America reports that anxiety disorder is the most common mental illness in the United States, affecting over 40 million adults[1].

What causes anxiety? I bet you can agree that the times you have experienced anxiety were when you either felt that things were out of your control or when you were uncertain about an outcome of something you expected. When we don't know what to lean on or who to go to for help, we begin to fear, panic, and get depressed; we suffer what has become customary in today's age - anxiety attack.

Trusting in God is the antidote to fear, worry, anxiety, panic, and depression. When we trust God, we become strength all around: We become mentally, physically, emotionally, and spiritually fit.

Through the Prophet Jeremiah, God said, *"Blessed is the man who trusts in the Lord, and whose hope is the Lord. For he shall be like a tree planted by the waters, which spreads out its roots by the river, and will not fear when heat comes; But its leaf will be green and will not be anxious in the year of drought, Nor will cease from yielding fruit"* Jeremiah 17:8.

---

[1] "Facts & Statistics," Anxiety and Depression Association of America, ADAA, accessed January 6, 2021, https://adaa.org/about-adaa/press-room/facts-statistics.

But how do we trust in the Lord? By being anxious for nothing, praying for everything, and giving thanks to the Lord. When we do this, the peace of God, which you won't understand, will guard your hearts and minds through Christ Jesus. So, live a God-dependent life by trusting in the Lord with all your heart, leaning not on your understanding (strength). In all your ways, concede to God. When you do this, God will direct (make smooth or straight) your paths (Proverbs 3:5-6).

Reflection

- Have you allowed the cares of this world, such as food, rent, or even approval by people, to make you put your trust in people?
- Imagine, how much of your mental space and energy would you save if you wholly depended on God?

88

Your Fellowship. Your Fulfilment

"...Enoch walked with God three hundred years and had sons and daughters... And Enoch walked with God; and he was not, for God took him" Genesis 5:22-24.

Enoch's name evokes admiration and inspiration because of the fellowship he had with God. The very few verses in scripture that talk about him only add to our desire to understand how God could walk with a man until He decided to take him alive. But would the way we admire and desire to understand Enoch's story, the way his close fellowship with God inspires us, be telling us something about our heart, its basic need?

The remarkable thing that stands out in Enoch's story is his walk with God, or in other words, the fellowship he enjoyed. And since the connection between God and Enoch (a man like us) is something we all desire, it is safe to conclude that fellowship with God is a significant source of our fulfillment.

Before man fell at the Garden of Eden, a significant thing we see is God coming to the garden and asking where Adam was (Genesis 3:8-9). God coming in search of man shows that God and man were having routine fellowship. Fellowship between God and man is a central theme throughout scripture. And this can make us safely conclude that we get fulfilled when we are in fellowship with God and the body of Christ.

When we look at Enoch's life, we find the key to having fellowship with God, faith. From Hebrews 11:5, we read, *"By faith, Enoch was taken away so that he did not see death, and was not found, because God had taken him; for before he was taken, he had this testimony, that he pleased God."* Therefore, the three Fs to keep in mind are Faith, Fellowship, and Fulfillment.

Reflection

- Jesus came into the world and died to restore our connection (fellowship) with God like it was before sin. Sin is what breaks our fellowship with God. Have you allowed Jesus to take away your sin? Are you walking in the righteousness of Christ, which assures fellowship?

89

Your Productivity, Your Fulfilment

"Be fruitful and multiply; fill the earth and subdue it; have dominion over the fish of the sea, over the birds of the air, and over every living thing that moves on the earth" Genesis 1:28.

The two desires in us that trace their origins from the beginning of time are a desire for fulfillment and fellowship. It's important to note that before God instructed us to be fruitful, He blessed us. Because of this act, God blessing man and ordering him to be fruitful, every man/woman can only be fulfilled if he or she becomes fruitful or productive. It means that God connected our fulfillment to our productivity.

The scriptures express the importance of fruitfulness. In the first Psalm of David, we get to see the recipe of how to be fruitful and also get to see what makes the difference between being fruitful and unfruitful.

The recipe is, delighting in the law of the Lord and meditating on it day and night. David compares such a man to a tree planted by the rivers of water, that brings forth its fruit in its season, and whose leaves never withers. The difference-maker, between fruitful or unfruitful, is where the man walks, stands, or sits.

Isaiah 35:8 says that the fruitful walk on the highway of Holiness. Romans 5:2 shows he stands in faith and grace and sits at the feet of Jesus according to Luke 10:39. On the contrary, unfruitful people walk in the counsel of the ungodly, stand in the path of sinners, and sit in the seat of the scornful.

So, to be fulfilled, you must be productive, and to be productive, you must examine your walk, where you stand and sit because they influence your delight and meditation.

Reflection

- Where are you standing, sitting, and walking? Who we surround ourselves with impacts our thoughts and actions! To be fully productive, we must choose our company carefully.
- Every day, ask yourself these questions: Am I producing according to my capacity? Is my circle of influence helping me to be a better producer?

90

Source Of Permanent Satisfaction

Have you ever noticed that the world offers solutions that require constant fixing? Often when we go to the doctor, we get treated for the symptoms and not the root cause, and the medications come with a certain number of refills attached to them. When a new technology arrives, we tend to think that it is the most superior. But it has proved challenging to keep up with the latest phones, TVs, and cars. All this is pointing to the truth that there are no real solutions that the world can offer, particularly solutions that meet our hearts' desires.

The passage of Jesus and the Samaritan woman gives more light to this truth (John 4:1-42). The woman could not satisfy her desires even after having been with six men. A daily walk to the well only kept her thirstier. She had depended on her traditions, the well of Jacob, and worshiping on the mountain to meet her physical and spiritual desires. She had never known of a better solution to her internal thirst until Jesus told her, *"The water that I shall give will become a fountain of water springing up into everlasting life."*

The Samaritan woman and her condition speak a lot about our hearts' conditions as well. We try to look for our souls' satisfaction in people and places we should not. Like her, we want new and exciting things that only fulfill our physical needs. But until we come to Jesus, who is the source of permanent satisfaction, we will always be thirsty.

We should always be willing to say to Jesus like the woman, *"Sir, give me this water, that I may not thirst, nor come here to draw."* So that we don't try to satisfy our heart's desire with things that pass away but get permanent satisfaction in Christ our Lord.

Reflection

- What does your heart desire to have? The Bible says that the heart is evil (Jeremiah 17:9), which means that our hearts can mislead us on what we should desire.
- How do you gauge your heart's desires?

91

Equipped And Loaded For Victory (Bonus)

If you stepped into a car dealership to purchase a new car, the dealer would ask you what features you want to be in your vehicle to narrow down your car selection. He would probably ask you whether you want a fully-loaded car or a standard one. In case you aren't aware, all vehicles, even the same model and make, are never the same; they differ in features and functions. If you drove behind a car, you might recognize the letters, LE, SE, and XLE, showing a fully-loaded car or a standard vehicle.

Unlike our creator, God, an automobile manufacturer, will decide on which features to have or have not in a car based on the end user's purchasing power. When God created you, he did not leave out some features because he thought you might not have the means to pay for your fully equipped you. He went all out in designing and equipping you with features and functions for your victorious living here on earth.

To start with, here is what God said when he was drawing your blueprint, *"Let Us make man in Our image, according to Our likeness; let them have dominion over the fish of the sea, over the birds of the air, and over the cattle, over all the earth and over every creeping thing that creeps on the earth"* Genesis 1:26.

Then Apostle Paul reveals to us that God did not only create us and leave us to figure out everything but made available His word that will continually update our software. He said, *"All Scripture is given by inspiration of God, and is profitable for doctrine, for reproof, for correction, for instruction in righteousness, that the man of God may be complete, thoroughly equipped for every good work"* 2 Timothy 3:16-17.

Because you are in the image and likeness of God, and you have His word, I am convinced that you are equipped and loaded for a victorious life. God enables us to live victoriously.

<u>Reflection</u>

- What would happen if you fully leaned on God? How would you live knowing the creator of the universe is backing you up and rooting for you to live a full life in Him?
- Do you know Jesus? Have you accepted Him as the only begotten Son of God? Because, outside of Jesus, it is impossible to live a victorious life. Make Jesus your friend and savior; Your life will never be the same again.
- *May the peace of God be with you.*

www.ingramcontent.com/pod-product-compliance
Lightning Source LLC
Chambersburg PA
CBHW071355290426

44108CB00014B/1559